Revolutionary Documents

From the Declaration of Independence to the
Confederate States of America Constitution

Works of the Public Domain

ISBN-13: 978- 1973850571
ISBN-10: 1973850575

CONTENTS

Editor's Note

These documents have been chosen for this book for an explicate purpose. As an American it is important to remember, our nation, was founded by rebels and rabble rousers. While I cannot agree with every word, it is important to know our history. I have chosen these specific writings to document our nation's history and heritage. These documents have been the cause for what is our nation and to know them is an essential part of what makes our nation what it is.

When in the course of human events, it becomes necessary for one people to dissolve the political bands which have connected them with another, and to assume among the powers of the earth, the separate and equal station to which the laws of nature and of nature's God entitle them, a decent respect to the opinions of mankind requires that they should declare the causes which impel them to the separation.

We hold these truths to be self-evident:

That all men are created equal; that they are endowed by their Creator with certain unalienable rights; that among these are life, liberty, and the pursuit of happiness; that, to secure these rights, governments are instituted among men, deriving their just powers from the consent of the governed; that whenever any form of government becomes destructive of these ends, it is the right of the people to alter or to abolish it, and to institute new government, laying its foundation on such principles, and organizing its powers in such form, as to them shall seem most likely to effect their safety and happiness. Prudence, indeed, will dictate that governments long established should not be changed for light and transient causes; and accordingly all experience hath shown that mankind are more disposed to suffer, while evils are sufferable than to right themselves by abolishing the forms to which they are accustomed. But when a long train of abuses and usurpations, pursuing invariably the same object, evinces a design to reduce them under absolute despotism, it is their right, it is their duty, to throw off such government, and to provide new guards for their future security. Such has been the patient sufferance of these colonies; and such is now the necessity which constrains them to alter their former systems of government. The history of the present King of Great Britain is a history of repeated injuries and usurpations, all having in direct object the establishment of an absolute tyranny over these states. To prove this, let facts be submitted to a candid world.

He has refused his assent to laws, the most wholesome and necessary for the public good.

He has forbidden his governors to pass laws of immediate and pressing importance, unless suspended in their operation till his assent should be obtained; and, when so suspended, he has utterly neglected to attend to them.

He has refused to pass other laws for the accommodation of large districts of people, unless those people would relinquish the right of representation in the legislature, a right inestimable to them, and formidable to tyrants only.

He has called together legislative bodies at places unusual uncomfortable, and distant from the depository of their public records, for the sole purpose of fatiguing them into compliance with his measures.

He has dissolved representative houses repeatedly, for opposing, with manly firmness, his invasions on the rights of the people.

He has refused for a long time, after such dissolutions, to cause others to be elected; whereby the legislative powers, incapable of annihilation, have returned to the people at large for their exercise; the state remaining, in the mean time, exposed to all the dangers of invasions from without and convulsions within.

He has endeavored to prevent the population of these states; for that purpose obstructing the laws for naturalization of foreigners; refusing to pass others to encourage their migration hither, and raising the conditions of new appropriations of lands.

He has obstructed the administration of justice, by refusing his assent to laws for establishing judiciary powers.

He has made judges dependent on his will alone, for the tenure of their offices, and the amount and payment of their salaries.

He has erected a multitude of new offices, and sent hither swarms of officers to harass our people and eat out their substance.

He has kept among us, in times of peace, standing armies, without the consent of our legislatures.

He has affected to render the military independent of, and superior to, the civil power.

He has combined with others to subject us to a jurisdiction foreign to our Constitution and unacknowledged by our laws, giving his assent to their acts of pretended legislation:

For quartering large bodies of armed troops among us;

For protecting them, by a mock trial, from punishment for any murders which they should commit on the inhabitants of these states;

For cutting off our trade with all parts of the world;

For imposing taxes on us without our consent;

For depriving us, in many cases, of the benefits of trial by jury;

For transporting us beyond seas, to be tried for pretended offenses;

For abolishing the free system of English laws in a neighboring province, establishing therein an arbitrary government, and enlarging its boundaries, so as to render it at once an example and fit instrument for introducing the same absolute rule into these colonies;

For taking away our charters, abolishing our most valuable laws, and altering fundamentally the forms of our governments;

For suspending our own legislatures, and declaring themselves invested with power to legislate for us in all cases whatsoever.

He has abdicated government here, by declaring us out of his protection and waging war against us.

He has plundered our seas, ravaged our coasts, burned our towns, and destroyed the lives of our people.

He is at this time transporting large armies of foreign mercenaries to complete the works of death, desolation, and tyranny already begun with circumstances of cruelty and perfidy scarcely paralleled in the most barbarous ages, and totally unworthy the head of a civilized nation.

He has constrained our fellow-citizens, taken captive on the high seas, to bear arms against their country, to become the executioners of their friends and brethren, or to fall themselves by their hands.

He has excited domestic insurrection among us, and has endeavored to bring on the inhabitants of our frontiers the merciless Indian savages, whose known rule of warfare is an undistinguished destruction of all ages, sexes, and conditions.

In every stage of these oppressions we have petitioned for redress in the most humble terms; our repeated petitions have been answered only by repeated injury. A prince, whose character is thus marked by every act which may define a tyrant, is unfit to be the ruler of a free people.

Nor have we been wanting in our attentions to our British brethren. We have warned them, from time to time, of attempts by their legislature to extend an unwarrantable jurisdiction over us. We have reminded them of the circumstances of our emigration and settlement here. We have appealed to their native justice and magnanimity; and we have conjured them, by the ties of our common kindred, to disavow these usurpations which would inevitably interrupt our connections and correspondence. They too, have been deaf to the voice of justice and of consanguinity. We must, therefore, acquiesce in the necessity which denounces our separation, and hold them as we hold the rest of mankind, enemies in war, in peace friends.

We, therefore, the representatives of the United States of America, in General Congress assembled, appealing to the Supreme Judge of the world for the rectitude of our intentions, do, in the name and by the authority of the good people of these colonies solemnly publish and declare, That these United Colonies are, and of right ought to be, FREE AND INDEPENDENT STATES; that they are absolved from all allegiance to the British crown and that all political connection between them and the state of Great Britain is, and ought to be, totally dissolved; and that, as free and independent states, they have full power to levy war, conclude peace, contract alliances, establish commerce, and do all other acts and things which independent states may of right do. And for the support of this declaration, with a firm reliance on the protection of Divine Providence, we mutually pledge to each other our lives, our fortunes, and our sacred honor.

[Signed by]

JOHN HANCOCK [President]

New Hampshire
JOSIAH BARTLETT,
WM. WHIPPLE,
MATTHEW THORNTON.

Massachusetts Bay
SAML. ADAMS,
JOHN ADAMS,
ROBT TREAT PAINE,
ELBRIDGE GERRY

Rhode Island
STEP. HOPKINS,
WILLIAM ELLERY.

Connecticut
ROGER SHERMAN,
SAM'EL HUNTINGTON,
WM. WILLIAMS,
OLIVER WOLCOTT.

New York
WM. FLOYD,
PHIL LIVINGSTON,
FRANS LEWIS,
LEWIS MORRIS.

New Jersey
RICHD STOCKTON,
JNO. WITHERSPOON,
FRAS. HOPKINSON,
JOHN HART,
ABRA CLARK.

Pennsylvania
ROBT. MORRIS
BENJAMIN RUSH,
BENJA. FRANKLIN,
JOHN MORTON,
GEO. CLYMER,
JAS. SMITH,
GEO. TAYLOR,
JAMES WILSON,
GEO. ROSS.

Delaware

CAESAR RODNEY,
GEO. READ,
THO. M'KEAN.

Maryland
SAMUEL CHASE,
WM. PACA,
THOS. STONE,
CHARLES CARROLL of Carrollton.

Virginia
GEORGE WYTHE,
RICHARD HENRY LEE,
TH. JEFFERSON,
BENJA. HARRISON,
THS. NELSON, JR.,
FRANCIS LIGHTFOOT LEE,
CARTER BRAXTON.

North Carolina
WM. HOOPER,
JOSEPH HEWES,
JOHN PENN.

South Carolina
EDWARD RUTLEDGE,
THOS. HAYWARD, JUNR.,
THOMAS LYNCH, JUNR.,
ARTHUR MIDDLETON.

Georgia
BUTTON GWINNETT,
LYMAN HALL,
GEO. WALTON

NOTE. - Mr. Ferdinand Jefferson, Keeper of the Rolls in the Department of State, at Washington, says: " The names of the signers are spelt above as in the facsimile of the original, but the punctuation of them is not always the same; neither do the names of the States appear in the facsimile of the original. The names of the signers of each State are grouped together in the facsimile of the original, except the name of Matthew Thornton, which follows that of Oliver Wolcott." - Revised Statutes of the United States, 2d edition, 1878, p. 6.

To all to whom these Presents shall come, we the undersigned Delegates of the States affixed to our Names send greeting.

Articles of Confederation and perpetual Union between the states of New Hampshire, Massachusetts-bay Rhode Island and Providence Plantations, Connecticut, New York, New Jersey, Pennsylvania, Delaware, Maryland, Virginia, North Carolina, South Carolina and Georgia.

I.

The Stile of this Confederacy shall be

"The United States of America".

II.

Each state retains its sovereignty, freedom, and independence, and every power, jurisdiction, and right, which is not by this Confederation expressly delegated to the United States, in Congress assembled.

III.

The said States hereby severally enter into a firm league of friendship with each other, for their common defense, the security of their liberties, and their mutual and general welfare, binding themselves to assist each other, against all force offered to, or attacks made upon them, or any of them, on account of religion, sovereignty, trade, or any other pretense whatever.

IV.

The better to secure and perpetuate mutual friendship and intercourse among the people of the different States in this Union, the free inhabitants of each of these States, paupers, vagabonds, and fugitives from justice excepted, shall be entitled to all privileges and immunities of free citizens in the several States; and the people of each State shall free ingress and regress to and from any other State, and shall enjoy therein all the privileges of trade and commerce, subject to the same duties, impositions, and restrictions as the inhabitants thereof respectively, provided that such restrictions shall not extend so far as to prevent the removal of property imported into any State, to any other State, of which the owner is an inhabitant; provided also that no imposition, duties or restriction shall be laid by any State, on the property of the United States, or either of them.

If any person guilty of, or charged with, treason, felony, or other high misdemeanor in any State, shall flee from justice, and be found in any of the United States, he shall, upon demand of the Governor or executive power of the State from which he fled, be delivered up and removed to the State having jurisdiction of his offense.

Full faith and credit shall be given in each of these States to the records, acts, and judicial proceedings of the courts and magistrates of every other State.

V.

For the most convenient management of the general interests of the United States, delegates shall be annually appointed in such manner as the legislatures of each State shall direct, to meet in Congress on the first Monday in November, in every year, with a powerreserved to each State to recall its delegates, or any of them, at any time within the year, and to send others in their stead for the remainder of the year.

No State shall be represented in Congress by less than two, nor more than seven members; and no person shall be capable of being a delegate for more than three years in any term of six years; nor shall any person, being a delegate, be capable of holding any office under the United States, for which he, or another for his benefit, receives any salary, fees or emolument of any kind.

Each State shall maintain its own delegates in a meeting of the States, and while they act as members of the committee of the States.

In determining questions in the United States in Congress assembled, each State shall have one vote.

Freedom of speech and debate in Congress shall not be impeached or questioned in any court or place out of Congress, and the members of Congress shall be protected in their persons from arrests or imprisonments, during the time of their going to and from, and attendence on Congress, except for treason, felony, or breach of the peace.

VI.

No State, without the consent of the United States in Congress assembled, shall send any embassy to, or receive any embassy from, or enter into any conference, agreement, alliance or treaty with any King, Prince or State; nor shall any person holding any office of profit or trust under the United States, or any of them, accept any present, emolument, office or title of any kind whatever from any King, Prince or foreign State; nor shall the United States in Congress assembled, or any of them, grant any title of nobility.

No two or more States shall enter into any treaty, confederation or alliance whatever between them, without the consent of the United States in Congress assembled, specifying accurately the purposes for which the same is to be entered into, and how long it shall continue.

No State shall lay any imposts or duties, which may interfere with any stipulations in treaties, entered into by the United States in Congress assembled, with any King, Prince or State, in pursuance of any treaties already proposed by Congress, to the courts of France and Spain.

No vessel of war shall be kept up in time of peace by any State, except such number only, as shall be deemed necessary by the United States in Congress assembled, for the defense of such State, or its trade; nor shall any body of forces be kept up by any State in time of peace, except such number only, as in the judgement of the United States in Congress assembled, shall be deemed requisite to garrison the forts necessary for the defense of such State; but every State shall always keep up a well-regulated and disciplined militia, sufficiently armed and accoutered, and shall provide and constantly have ready for use, in public stores, a due number of filed pieces and tents, and a proper quantity of arms, ammunition and camp equipage.

No State shall engage in any war without the consent of the United States in Congress assembled, unless such State be actually invaded by enemies, or shall have received certain advice of a resolution being formed by some nation of Indians to invade such State, and the danger is so imminent as not to admit of a delay till the United States in Congress assembled can be consulted; nor shall any State grant commissions to any ships or vessels of war, nor letters of marque or reprisal, except it be after a declaration of war by the United States in Congress assembled, and then only against the Kingdom or State and the subjects thereof, against which war has been so declared, and under such regulations as shall be established by the United States in Congress assembled, unless such State be infested by pirates, in which case vessels of war may be fitted out for that occasion, and kept so long as the danger shall continue, or until the United States in Congress assembled shall determine otherwise.

VII.

When land forces are raised by any State for the common defense, all officers of or under the rank of colonel, shall be appointed by the legislature of each State respectively, by whom such forces shall be raised, or in such manner as such State shall direct, and all vacancies shall be filled up by the State which first made the appointment.

VIII.

All charges of war, and all other expenses that shall be incurred for the
common defense or general welfare, and allowed by the United States
in Congress assembled, shall be defrayed out of a common treasury,
which shall be supplied by the several States in proportion to the value
of all land within each State, granted or surveyed for any person, as
such land and the buildings and improvements thereon shall be
estimated according to such mode as the United States in Congress
assembled, shall from time to time direct and appoint.

The taxes for paying that proportion shall be laid and levied by the
authority and direction of the legislatures of the several States within
the time agreed upon by the United States in Congress assembled.

IX.

The United States in Congress assembled, shall have the sole and
exclusive right and power of determining on peace and war, except in
the cases mentioned in the sixth article -- of sending and receiving
ambassadors -- entering into treaties and alliances, provided that no
treaty of commerce shall be made whereby the legislative power of the
respective States shall be restrained from imposing such imposts and
duties on foreigners, as their own people are subjected to, or from
prohibiting the exportation or importation of any species of goods or
commodities whatsoever -- of establishing rules for deciding in all
cases, what captures on land or water shall be legal, and in what
manner prizes taken by land or naval forces in the service of the
United States shall be divided or appropriated -- of granting letters of
marque and reprisal in times of peace -- appointing courts for the trial
of piracies and felonies commited on the high seas and establishing
courts for receiving and determining finally appeals in all cases of
captures, provided that no member of Congress shall be appointed a
judge of any of the said courts.

The United States in Congress assembled shall also be the last resort on appeal in all disputes and differences now subsisting or that hereafter may arise between two or more States concerning boundary, jurisdiction or any other causes whatever; which authority shall always be exercised in the manner following. Whenever the legislative or executive authority or lawful agent of any State in controversy with another shall present a petition to Congress stating the matter in question and praying for a hearing, notice thereof shall be given by order of Congress to the legislative or executive authority of the other State in controversy, and a day assigned for the appearance of the parties by their lawful agents, who shall then be directed to appoint by joint consent, commissioners or judges to constitute a court for hearing and determining the matter in question: but if they cannot agree, Congress shall name three persons out of each of the United States, and from the list of such persons each party shall alternately strike out one, the petitioners beginning, until the number shall be reduced to thirteen; and from that number not less than seven, nor more than nine names as Congress shall direct, shall in the presence of Congress be drawn out by lot, and the persons whose names shall be so drawn or any five of them, shall be commissioners or judges, to hear and finally determine the controversy, so always as a major part of the judges who shall hear the cause shall agree in the determination: and if either party shall neglect to attend at the day appointed, without showing reasons, which Congress shall judge sufficient, or being present shall refuse to strike, the Congress shall proceed to nominate three persons out of each State, and the secretary of Congress shall strike in behalf of such party absent or refusing; and the judgement and sentence of the court to be appointed, in the manner before prescribed, shall be final and conclusive; and if any of the parties shall refuse to submit to the authority of such court, or to appear or defend their claim or cause, the court shall nevertheless proceed to pronounce sentence, or judgement, which shall in like manner be final and decisive, the judgement or sentence and other proceedings being in either case transmitted to Congress, and lodged among the acts of Congress for the security of the parties concerned: provided that every commissioner, before he sits in judgement, shall take an oath to be administered by one of the judges of the supreme or superior court of the State, where the cause shall be tried, 'well and truly to hear and determine the matter in question, according to the best of his judgement, without favor, affection or hope of reward': provided also, that no State shall be deprived of territory for the benefit of the United States.

All controversies concerning the private right of soil claimed under different grants of two or more States, whose jurisdictions as they may respect such lands, and the States which passed such grants are adjusted, the said grants or either of them being at the same time claimed to have originated antecedent to such settlement of jurisdiction, shall on the petition of either party to the Congress of the United States, be finally determined as near as may be in the same manner as is before presecribed for deciding disputes respecting territorial jurisdiction between different States.

The United States in Congress assembled shall also have the sole and exclusive right and power of regulating the alloy and value of coin struck by their own authority, or by that of the respective States -- fixing the standards of weights and measures throughout the United States -- regulating the trade and managing all affairs with the Indians, not members of any of the States, provided that the legislative right of any State within its own limits be not infringed or violated -- establishing or regulating post offices from one State to another, throughout all the United States, and exacting such postage on the papers passing through the same as may be requisite to defray the expenses of the said office -- appointing all officers of the land forces, in the service of the United States, excepting regimental officers -- appointing all the officers of the naval forces, and commissioning all officers whatever in the service of the United States -- making rules for the government and regulation of the said land and naval forces, and directing their operations.

The United States in Congress assembled shall have authority to appoint a committee, to sit in the recess of Congress, to be denominated 'A Committee of the States', and to consist of one delegate from each State; and to appoint such other committees and civil officers as may be necessary for managing the general affairs of the United States under their direction -- to appoint one of their members to preside, provided that no person be allowed to serve in the office of president more than one year in any term of three years; to ascertain the necessary sums of money to be raised for the service of the United States, and to appropriate and apply the same for defraying the public expenses -- to borrow money, or emit bills on the credit of the United States, transmitting every half-year to the respective States an account of the sums of money so borrowed or emitted -- to build and equip a navy -- to agree upon the number of land forces, and to make requisitions from each State for its quota, in proportion to the number of white inhabitants in such State; which requisition shall be binding, and thereupon the legislature of each State shall appoint the regimental officers, raise the men and cloath, arm and equip them in a solid-like manner, at the expense of the United States; and the officers and men so cloathed, armed and equipped shall march to the place appointed, and within the time agreed on by the United States in Congress assembled. But if the United States in Congress assembled shall, on consideration of circumstances judge proper that any State should not raise men, or should raise a smaller number of men than the quota thereof, such extra number shall be raised, officered, cloathed, armed and equipped in the same manner as the quota of each State, unless the legislature of such State shall judge that such extra number cannot be safely spread out in the same, in which case they shall raise, officer, cloath, arm and equip as many of such extra number as they judeg can be safely spared. And the officers and men so cloathed, armed, and equipped, shall march to the place appointed, and within the time agreed on by the United States in Congress assembled.

The United States in Congress assembled shall never engage in a war, nor grant letters of marque or reprisal in time of peace, nor enter into any treaties or alliances, nor coin money, nor regulate the value thereof, nor ascertain the sums and expenses necessary for the defense and welfare of the United States, or any of them, nor emit bills, nor borrow money on the credit of the United States, nor appropriate money, nor agree upon the number of vessels of war, to be built or purchased, or the number of land or sea forces to be raised, nor appoint a commander in chief of the army or navy, unless nine States assent to the same: nor shall a question on any other point, except for adjourning from day to day be determined, unless by the votes of the majority of the United States in Congress assembled.

The Congress of the United States shall have power to adjourn to any time within the year, and to any place within the United States, so that no period of adjournment be for a longer duration than the space of six months, and shall publish the journal of their proceedings monthly, except such parts thereof relating to treaties, alliances or military operations, as in their judgement require secrecy; and the yeas and nays of the delegates of each State on any question shall be entered on the journal, when it is desired by any delegates of a State, or any of them, at his or their request shall be furnished with a transcript of the said journal, except such parts as are above excepted, to lay before the legislatures of the several States.

X.

The Committee of the States, or any nine of them, shall be authorized to execute, in the recess of Congress, such of the powers of Congress as the United States in Congress assembled, by the consent of the nine States, shall from time to time think expedient to vest them with; provided that no power be delegated to the said Committee, for the exercise of which, by the Articles of Confederation, the voice of nine States in the Congress of the United States assembled be requisite.

XI.

Canada acceding to this confederation, and adjoining in the measures of the United States, shall be admitted into, and entitled to all the advantages of this Union; but no other colony shall be admitted into the same, unless such admission be agreed to by nine States.

XII.

All bills of credit emitted, monies borrowed, and debts contracted by, or under the authority of Congress, before the assembling of the United States, in pursuance of the present confederation, shall be deemed and considered as a charge against the United States, for payment and satisfaction whereof the said United States, and the public faith are hereby solemnly pleged.

XIII.

Every State shall abide by the determination of the United States in Congress assembled, on all questions which by this confederation are submitted to them. And the Articles of this Confederation shall be inviolably observed by every State, and the Union shall be perpetual; nor shall any alteration at any time hereafter be made in any of them; unless such alteration be agreed to in a Congress of the United States, and be afterwards confirmed by the legislatures of every State.

And Whereas it hath pleased the Great Governor of the World to incline the hearts of the legislatures we respectively represent in Congress, to approve of, and to authorize us to ratify the said Articles of Confederation and perpetual Union. Know Ye that we the undersigned delegates, by virtue of the power and authority to us given for that purpose, do by these presents, in the name and in behalf of our respective constituents, fully and entirely ratify and confirm each and every of the said Articles of Confederation and perpetual Union, and all and singular the matters and things therein contained: And we do further solemnly plight and engage the faith of our respective constituents, that they shall abide by the determinations of the United States in Congress assembled, on all questions, which by the said Confederation are submitted to them. And that the Articles thereof shall be inviolably observed by the States we respectively represent, and that the Union shall be perpetual.

In Witness whereof we have hereunto set our hands in Congress.
Done at Philadelphia in the State of Pennsylvania the ninth day of July
in the Year of our Lord One Thousand Seven Hundred and Seventy-
Eight, and in the Third Year of the independence of America.

Agreed to by Congress 15 November 1777 In force after ratification
by Maryland, 1 March 1781

Constitution of the United States : June 21, 1788

Preamble

We, the people of the United States, in order to form a more perfect
Union, establish justice, insure domestic tranquility, provide for the
common defense, promote the general welfare, and secure the
blessings of liberty to ourselves and our posterity, do ordain and
establish this Constitution for the United States of America.

Article I

Section 1 - Legislative powers; in whom vested

All legislative powers herein granted shall be vested in a Congress of
the United States, which shall consist of a Senate and House of
Representatives.

Section 2 - House of Representatives, how and by whom chosen
Qualifications of a Representative. Representatives and direct taxes,
how apportioned. Enumeration. Vacancies to be filled. Power of
choosing officers, and of impeachment.

1. The House of Representatives shall be composed of members
chosen every second year by the people of the several States, and the
elector in each State shall have the qualifications requisite for electors
of the most numerous branch of the State Legislature.

2. No person shall be a Representative who shall not have attained the
age of twenty-five years, and been seven years a Citizen of the United
States, and who shall not, when elected, be an inhabitant of that State
in which he shall be chosen.

3. Representatives and direct taxes shall be apportioned among the
several States which may be included within this Union, according to
their respective numbers, which shall be determined by adding the

whole number of free persons, including those bound to service for a term of years, and excluding Indians not taxed, three-fifths of all other persons.(The previous sentence was superseded by Amendment XIV). The actual enumeration shall be made within three years after the first meeting of the Congress of the United States, and within every subsequent term of ten years, in such manner as they shall by law direct. The number of Representatives shall not exceed one for every thirty thousand, but each State shall have at least one Representative; and until such enumeration shall be made, the State of New Hampshire shall be entitled to choose three, Massachusetts eight, Rhode Island and Providence Plantations one, Connecticut five, New York six, New Jersey four, Pennsylvania eight, Delaware one, Maryland six, Virginia ten, North Carolina five, South Carolina five, and Georgia three.

4. When vacancies happen in the representation from any State, the Executive Authority thereof shall issue writs of election to fill such vacancies.

5. The House of Representatives shall choose their Speaker and other officers; and shall have the sole power of impeachment.

Section 3 - Senators, how and by whom chosen. How classified. State Executive, when to make temporary appointments, in case, etc. Qualifications of a Senator. President of the Senate, his right to vote. President pro tem., and other officers of the Senate, how chosen. Power to try impeachments. When President is tried, Chief Justice to preside. Sentence.

1. The Senate of the United States shall be composed of two Senators from each State, (chosen by the Legislature thereof,) (The preceding five words were superseded by Amendment XVII) for six years; and each Senator shall have one vote.

2. Immediately after they shall be assembled in consequence of the first election, they shall be divided as equally as may be into three classes.

The seats of the Senators of the first class shall be vacated at the expiration of the second year, of the second class at the expiration of the fourth year, and of the third class at the expiration of the sixth year, so that one-third may be chosen every second year; and if vacancies happen by resignation, or otherwise, during the recess of the Legislature of any State, the Executive thereof may make temporary appointments until the next meeting of the Legislature, which shall then fill such vacancies. (The words in italics were superseded by Amendment XVII)

3. No person shall be a Senator who shall not have attained to the age of thirty years, and been nine years a Citizen of the United States, and who shall not, when elected, be an inhabitant of that State for which he shall be chosen.

4. The Vice-President of the United States shall be President of the Senate, but shall have no vote, unless they be equally divided.

5. The Senate shall choose their other officers, and also a President pro tempore, in the absence of the Vice President, or when he shall exercise the office of the President of the United States.

6. The Senate shall have the sole power to try all impeachments. When sitting for that purpose, they shall be on oath or affirmation. When the President of the United States is tried, the Chief Justice shall preside: and no person shall be convicted without the concurrence of two-thirds of the members present.

7. Judgement in cases of impeachment shall not extend further than to removal from office, and disqualification to hold and enjoy any office of honor, trust, or profit under the United States: but the party convicted shall nevertheless be liable and subject to indictment, trial, judgement and punishment, according to law.

Section 4 - Times, etc., of holding elections, how prescribed. One session in each year.

1. The times, places and manner of holding elections for Senators and Representatives, shall be prescribed in each State by the Legislature thereof; but the Congress may at any time by law make or alter such regulations, except as to the places of choosing Senators.

2. The Congress shall assemble at least once in every year, and such meeting shall be on the first Monday in December,(The words in italics were superseded by Amendment XX) unless they by law appoint a different day.

Section 5 - Membership, Quorum, Adjournments, Rules, Power to punish or expel. Journal. Time of adjournments, how limited, etc.

1. Each House shall be the judge of the elections, returns and qualifications of its own members, and a majority of each shall constitute a quorum to do business; but a smaller number may adjourn from day to day, and may be authorized to compel the attendance of absent members, in such manner, and under such penalties as each House may provide.

2. Each House may determine the rules of its proceedings, punish its members for disorderly behavior, and, with the concurrence of two-thirds, expel a member.

3. Each House shall keep a journal of its proceedings, and from time to time publish the same, excepting such parts as may in their judgement require secrecy; and the yeas and nays of the members of either House on any question shall, at the desire of one-fifth of those present, be entered on the journal.

4. Neither House, during the session of Congress, shall, without the consent of the other, adjourn for more than three days, nor to any other place than that in which the two Houses shall be sitting.

Section 6 - Compensation, Privileges, Disqualification in certain cases.

1. The Senators and Representatives shall receive a compensation for their services, to be ascertained by law, and paid out of the Treasury of the United States. They shall in all cases, except treason, felony and breach of the peace, be privileged from arrest during their attendance at the session of their respective Houses, and in going to and returning from the same; and for any speech or debate in either House, they shall not be questioned in any other place.

2. No Senator or Representative shall, during the time for which he was elected, be appointed to any civil office under the authority of the United States, which shall have increased during such time; and no person holding any office under the United States, shall be a member of either House during his continuance in office.

Section 7 - House to originate all revenue bills. Veto. Bill may be passed by two-thirds of each House, notwithstanding, etc. Bill, not returned in ten days to become a law. Provisions as to orders, concurrent resolutions, etc.

1. All bills for raising revenue shall originate in the House of Representatives; but the Senate may propose or concur with amendments as on other bills.

2. Every bill which shall have passed the House of Representatives and the Senate, shall, before it become a law, be presented to the president of the United States; if he approve, he shall sign it, but if not, he shall return it, with his objections, to that house in which it shall have originated, who shall enter the objections at large on their journal, and proceed to reconsider it. If after such reconsideration, two thirds of that house shall agree to pass the bill, it shall be sent, together with the objections, to the other house, by which it shall likewise be reconsidered, and if approved by two-thirds of that house, it shall become a law. But in all such cases the votes of both houses shall be determined by yeas and nays, and the names of the persons voting for and against the bill shall be entered on the journal of each house

respectively. If any bill shall not be returned by the president within ten days (Sundays excepted) after it shall have been presented to him, the same shall be a law, in like manner as if he had signed it, unless the Congress by their adjournment prevent its return, in which case it shall not be a law.

3. Every order, resolution, or vote to which the concurrence of the Senate and House of Representatives may be necessary (except on a question of adjournment) shall be presented to the president of the United States; and before the same shall take effect, shall be approved by him, or, being disapproved by him, shall be re-passed by two-thirds of the Senate and House of Representatives, according to the rules and limitations prescribed in the case of a bill.

Section 8 - Powers of Congress

The Congress shall have the power

1. To lay and collect taxes, duties, imposts and excises, to pay the debts and provide for the common defence and general welfare of the United States; but all duties, imposts and excises shall be uniform throughout the United States:

2. To borrow money on the credit of the United States:

3. To regulate commerce with foreign nations, and among the several states,and with the Indian tribes:

4. To establish an uniform rule of naturalization, and uniform laws on the subject of bankruptcies throughout the United States:

5. To coin money, regulate the value thereof, and of foreign coin, and fix the standard of weights and measures:

6. To provide for the punishment of counterfeiting the securities and current coin of the United States:

7. To establish post-offices and post-roads:

8. To promote the progress of science and useful arts, by securing for limited times to authors and inventors the exclusive right to their respective writings and discoveries:

9. To constitute tribunals inferior to the supreme court:

10. To define and punish piracies and felonies committed on the high seas, and offences against the law of nations:

11. To declare war, grant letters of marque and reprisal, and make rules concerning captures on land and water:

12. To raise and support armies, but no appropriation of money to that use shall be for a longer term than two years:

13. To provide and maintain a navy:

14. To make rules for the government and regulation of the land and naval forces:

15. To provide for calling forth the militia to execute the laws of the union, suppress insurrections and repel invasions:

16. To provide for organizing, arming and disciplining the militia, and for governing such part of them as may be employed in the service of the United States, reserving to the states respectively, the appointment of the officers, and the authority of training the militia according to the discipline prescribed by Congress:

17. To exercise exclusive legislation in all cases whatsoever, over such district (not exceeding ten miles square) as may, by cession of particular states, and the acceptance of Congress, become the seat of the government of the United States, and to exercise like authority

over all places purchased by the consent of the legislature of the state
in which the same shall be, for the erection of forts, magazines,
arsenals, dock-yards, and other needful buildings: And,

18. To make all laws which shall be necessary and proper for carrying
into execution the foregoing powers, and all other powers vested by
this constitution in the government of the United States, or in any
department or officer thereof.

Section 9 - Provision as to migration or importation of certain persons.
Habeas Corpus , Bills of attainder, etc. Taxes, how apportioned. No
export duty. No commercial preference. Money, how drawn from
Treasury, etc. No titular nobility. Officers not to receive presents, etc.

1. The migration or importation of such persons as any of the states
now existing shall think proper to admit, shall not be prohibited by the
Congress prior to the year 1808, but a tax or duty may be imposed on
such importations, not exceeding 10 dollars for each person.

2. The privilege of the writ of habeas corpus shall not be suspended,
unless when in cases of rebellion or invasion the public safety may
require it.

3. No bill of attainder or ex post facto law shall be passed.

4. No capitation, or other direct tax shall be laid unless in proportion
to the census or enumeration herein before directed to be taken.
(Modified by Amendement XVI)

5. No tax or duty shall be laid on articles exported from any state.

6. No preference shall be given by any regulation of commerce or
revenue to the ports of one state over those of another: nor shall
vessels bound to, or from one state, be obliged to enter, clear, or pay
duties in another.

7. No money shall be drawn from the treasury but in consequence of appropriations made by law; and a regular statement and account of the receipts and expenditures of all public money shall be published from time to time.

8. No title of nobility shall be granted by the United States: And no person holding any office or profit or trust under them, shall, without the consent of the Congress, accept of any present, emolument, office, or title, of any kind whatever, from any king, prince, or foreign state.

Section 10 - States prohibited from the exercise of certain powers.

1. No state shall enter into any treaty, alliance, or confederation; grant letters of marque and reprisal; coin money; emit bills of credit; make any thing but gold and silver coin a tender in payment of debts; pass any bill of attainder, ex post facto law, or law impairing the obligation of contracts, or grant any title of nobility.

2. No state shall, without the consent of the Congress, lay any imposts or duties on imports or exports, except what may be absolutely necessary for executing its inspection laws; and the net produce of all duties and imposts, laid by any state on imports or exports, shall be for the use of the treasury of the United States; and all such laws shall be subject to the revision and control of the Congress.

3. No state shall, without the consent of Congress, lay any duty of tonnage, keep troops, or ships of war in time of peace, enter into any agreement or compact with another state, or with a foreign power, or engage in a war, unless actually invaded, or in such imminent danger as will not admit of delay.

Article II

Section 1- President: his term of office. Electors of President; number and how appointed. Electors to vote on same day. Qualification of

President. On whom his duties devolve in case of his removal, death, etc. President's compensation. His oath of office.

1. The Executive power shall be vested in a President of the United States of America. He shall hold office during the term of four years, and together with the Vice President, chosen for the same term, be elected as follows:

2. Each State shall appoint, in such manner as the Legislature may direct, a number of electors, equal to the whole number of Senators and Representatives to which the State may be entitled in the Congress: but no Senator or Representative, or person holding an office of trust or profit under the United States, shall be appointed an elector. The electors shall meet in their respective States, and vote by ballot for two persons, of whom one at least shall not be an inhabitant of the same State with themselves. And they shall make a list of all the persons voted for each; which list they shall sign and certify, and transmit sealed to the seat of Government of the United States, directed to the President of the Senate. The President of the Senate shall, in the presence of the Senate and House of Representatives, open all the certificates, and the votes shall then be counted. The person having the greatest number of votes shall be the President, if such number be a majority of the whole number of electors appointed; and if there be more than one who have such majority, and have an equal number of votes, then the House of Representatives shall immediately choose by ballot one of them for President; and if no person have a majority, then from the five highest on the list the said House shall in like manner choose the President. But in choosing the President, the votes shall be taken by States, the representation from each State having one vote; a quorum for this purpose shall consist of a member or members from two-thirds of the States, and a majority of all the States shall be necessary to a choice. In every case, after the choice of the President, the person having the greatest number of votes of the electors shall be the Vice President. But if there should remain two or more who have equal votes, the Senate shall choose

from them by ballot the Vice President.(The clause in italics was superseded by Amendment XII)

3. The Congress may determine the time of choosing the electors, and the day on which they shall give their votes; which day shall be the same throughout the United States.

4. No person except a natural born Citizen, or a Citizen of the United States, at the time of the adoption of this Constitution, shall be eligible to the office of President; neither shall any person be eligible to that office who shall not have attained to the age of thirty-five years, and been fourteen years a resident within the United States.

5 . In case of the removal of the President from office, or of his death, resignation, or inability to discharge the powers and duties of the said office, the same shall devolve on the Vice President, and the Congress may by law provide for the case of removal, death, resignation, or inability, both of the President and Vice President, declaring what officer shall then act as President, and such officer shall act accordingly, until the disability be removed, or a President shall be elected. (This clause has been modified by Amendment XX and Amendment XXV)

6. The President shall, at stated times, receive for his services, a compensation, which shall neither be increased nor diminished during the period for which he shall have been elected, and he shall not receive within that period any other emolument from the United States, or any of them.

7. Before he enter on the execution of his office, he shall take the following oath or affirmation:
"I do solemnly swear (or affirm) that I will faithfully execute the office of the President of the United States, and will to the best of my ability, preserve, protect and defend the Constitution of the United States."

Section 2 - President to be Commander-in-Chief. He may require opinions of cabinet officers, etc., may pardon. Treaty-making power. Nomination of certain officers. When President may fill vacancies.

1. The President shall be Commander-in-Chief of the Army and Navy of the United States, and of the militia of the several States, when called into the actual service of the United States; he may require the opinion, in writing, of the principal officer in each of the executive departments, upon any subject relating to the duties of their respective offices, and he shall have power to grant reprieves and pardons for offenses against the United States, except in cases of impeachment.

2. He shall have power, by and with the advice and consent of the Senate, to make treaties, provided two-thirds of the Senators present concur; and he shall nominate, and by and with the advice and consent of the Senate, shall appoint ambassadors, other public ministers and consuls, judges of the Supreme Court, and all other officers of the United States, whose appointments are not herein otherwise provided for, and which shall be established by law: but the Congress may by law vest the appointment of such inferior officers, as they think proper, in the President alone, in the courts of law, or in the heads of departments.

3. The President shall have the power to fill up all vacancies that may happen during the recess of the Senate, by granting commissions, which shall expire at the end of their next session.

Section 3 - President shall communicate to Congress. He may convene and adjourn Congress, in case of disagreement, etc. Shall receive ambassadors, execute laws, and commission officers.

He shall from time to time give to the Congress information of the state of the Union, and recommend to their consideration such measures as he shall judge necessary and expedient; he may, on extraordinary occasions, convene both Houses, or either of them, and in case of disagreement between them, with respect to the time of

adjournment, he may adjourn them to such time as he shall think
proper; he may receive ambassadors, and other public ministers; he
shall take care that the laws be faithfully executed, and shall
commission all the officers of the United States.

4 - All civil offices forfeited for certain crimes.

The President, Vice President, and all civil officers of the United
States, shall be removed from office on impeachment for, and
conviction of, treason, bribery, or other high crimes and
misdemeanors.

Article III

Section 1- Judicial powers. Tenure. Compensation.

The judicial power of the United States, shall be vested in one supreme
court, and in such inferior courts as the Congress may, from time to
time, ordain and establish. The judges, both of the supreme and
inferior courts, shall hold their offices during good behaviour, and
shall, at stated times, receive for their services a compensation, which
shall not be diminished during their continuance in office.

Section 2 - Judicial power; to what cases it extends. Original
jurisdiction of Supreme Court Appellate. Trial by Jury, etc. Trial, where

1. The judicial power shall extend to all cases, in law and equity, arising
under this constitution, the laws of the United States, and treaties
made, or which shall be made under their authority; to all cases
affecting ambassadors, other public ministers and consuls; to all cases
of admiralty and maritime jurisdiction; to controversies to which the
United States shall be a party; to controversies between two or more
states, between a state and Citizens of another state, between Citizens
of different states, between Citizens of the same state, claiming lands
under grants of different states, and between a state, or the Citizens

thereof, and foreign states, Citizens or subjects. (This section modified by Amendment XI)

2. In all cases affecting ambassadors, other public ministers and consuls, and those in which a state shall be a party, the supreme court shall have original jurisdiction. In all the other cases before-mentioned, the supreme court shall have appellate jurisdiction, both as to law and fact, with such exceptions, and under such regulations as the Congress shall make.

3. The trial of all crimes, except in cases of impeachment, shall be by jury; and such trial shall be held in the state where the said crimes shall have been committed; but when not committed within any state, the trial shall be at such place or places as the Congress may by law have directed.

Section 3 - Treason defined. Proof of. Punishment of.

1. Treason against the United States shall consist only in levying war against them, or in adhering to their enemies, giving them aid and comfort. No person shall be convicted of treason unless on the testimony of two witnesses to the same overt act, or on confession in open court.

2. The Congress shall have power to declare the punishment of treason, but no attainder of treason shall work corruption of blood, or forfeiture, except during the life of the person attainted.

Article IV

Section 1 - Each State to give credit to the public acts, etc. of every other State.

Full faith and credit shall be given in each state to the public acts, records and judicial proceedings of every other state. And the

Congress may by general laws prescribe the manner in which such acts, records and proceedings shall be proved, and the effect thereof.

Section 2 - Privileges of Citizens of each State. Fugitives from Justice to be delivered up. Persons held to service having escaped, to be delivered up.

1. The Citizens of each state shall be entitled to all privileges and immunities of Citizens in the several states.

2. A person charged in any state with treason, felony, or other crime, who shall flee justice, and be found in another state, shall, on demand of the executive authority of the state from which he fled, be delivered up, to be removed to the state having jurisdiction of the crime.

3. No person held to service or labour in one state, under the laws thereof, escaping into another, shall, in consequence of any law or regulation therein, be discharged from such service or labour, but shall be delivered up on claim of the party to whom such service or labour may be due.(This clause superseded by Amendment XIII)

Section 3 - Admission of new States. Power of Congress over territory and other property.

1. New states may be admitted by the Congress into this union; but no new state shall be formed or erected within the jurisdiction of any other state, nor any state be formed by the junction of two or more states, without the consent of the legislatures of the states concerned, as well as of the Congress.

2. The Congress shall have power to dispose of and make all needful rules and regulations respecting the territory or other property belonging to the United States; and nothing in this constitution shall be so construed as to prejudice any claims of the United States, or of any particular state.

Section 4 - Republican form of government guaranteed. Each State to be protected.

The United States shall guarantee to every state in this union, a republican form of government, and shall protect each of them against invasion; and on application of the legislature, or of the executive (when the legislature cannot be convened), against domestic violence.

Article V

Constitution: how amended; proviso.

The Congress, whenever two-thirds of both houses shall deem it necessary, shall propose amendments to this constitution, or on the application of the legislatures of two-thirds of the several states, shall call a convention for proposing amendments, which , in either case, shall be valid to all intents and purposes, as part of this constitution, when ratified by the legislatures of three-fourths of the several states, or by conventions in three-fourths thereof, as the one or the other mode of ratification may be proposed by the Congress: Provided, that no amendment which may be made prior to the year 1808, shall in any manner affect the first and fourth clauses in the ninth section of the first article; and that no state, without its consent, shall be deprived of its equal suffrage in the Senate.

Article VI

Certain debts, ect. declared valid, Supremacy of Constitution, treaties, and laws of the United States, Oath to support Constitution, by whom taken. No religious test.

1. All debts contracted and engagements entered into, before the adoption of this constitution, shall be as valid against the United States under this constitution, as under the confederation.

2. This constitution, and the laws of the United States which shall be made in pursuance thereof; and all treaties made, or which shall be made, under the authority of the United States shall be the supreme law of the land; and the judges in every state shall be bound thereby, any thing in the constitution or laws of any state to the contrary notwithstanding.

3. The senators and representatives before-mentioned, and the members of the several state legislatures, and all executive and judicial officers, both of the United States and of the several states, shall be bound by oath or affirmation, to support this constitution; but no religious test shall ever be required as a qualification to any office or public trust under the United States.

Article VII

What ratification shall establish constitution.

The ratification of the conventions of nine states, shall be sufficient for the establishment of this constitution between the states so ratifying the same.

Bill of Rights - The First Ten Amendments

I - Freedom of Speech, Press, Religion and Petition

Congress shall make no law respecting an establishment of religion, or prohibiting the free exercise thereof; or abridging the freedom of speech, or of the press; or the right of the people peaceably to assemble, and to petition the Government for a redress of grievances.

II - Right to keep and bear arms

A well-regulated militia, being necessary to the security of a free State, the right of the people to keep and bear arms, shall not be infringed.

III - Conditions for quarters of soldiers

No soldier shall, in time of peace be quartered in any house, without the consent of the owner, nor in time of war, but in a manner to be prescribed by law.

IV - Right of search and seizure regulated

The right of the people to be secure in their persons, houses, papers, and effects, against unreasonable searches and seizures, shall not be violated, and no warrants shall issue, but upon probable cause, supported by oath or affirmation, and particularly describing the place to be searched, and the persons or things to be seized.

V - Provisons concerning prosecution

No person shall be held to answer for a capital, or otherwise infamous crime, unless on a presentment or indictment of a Grand Jury, except in cases arising in the land or naval forces, or in the militia, when in actual service in time of war or public danger; nor shall any person be subject for the same offense to be twice put in jeopardy of life or limb; nor shall be compelled in any criminal case to be a witness against himself, nor be deprived of life, liberty, or property, without due process of law; nor shall private property be taken for public use without just compensation.

VI - Right to a speedy trial, witnesses, etc.

In all criminal prosecutions, the accused shall enjoy the right to a speedy and public trial, by an impartial jury of the State and district wherein the crime shall have been committed, which district shall have been previously ascertained by law, and to be informed of the nature and cause of the accusation; to be confronted with the witnesses against him; to have compulsory process for obtaining witnesses in his favor, and to have the assistance of counsel for his defense.

VII - Right to a trial by jury

In suits at common law, where the value in controversy shall exceed twenty dollars, the right of trial by jury shall be preserved, and no fact tried by a jury shall be otherwise reexamined in any court of the United States, than according to the rules of the common law.

VIII - Excessive bail, cruel punishment

Excessive bail shall not be required, nor excessive fines imposed, nor cruel and unusual punishments inflicted.

IX - Rule of construction of Constitution

The enumeration in the Constitution, of certain rights, shall not be construed to deny or disparage others retained by the people.

X - Rights of the States under Constitution

The powers not delegated to the United States by the Constitution, nor prohibited by it to the States, are reserved to the States respectively, or to the people.

Amendments XI – XXVII

XI - Judicial Powers Construed

Passed by Congress March 4, 1794. Ratified February 7, 1795.

The judicial power of the United States shall not be construed to extend to any suit in law or equity, commenced or prosecuted against one of the United States by citizens of another State, or by citizens or subjects of any foreign state.

XII - Manner of Choosing a President and Vice-President

This Amendment altered Article 2 Section 1 Part 2

Passed by Congress December 9, 1803. Ratified July 27, 1804.

1. The Electors shall meet in their respective States and vote by ballot
for President and Vice-President, one of whom, at least, shall not be an
inhabitant of the same State with themselves; they shall name in their
ballots the person voted for as President, and in distinct ballots the
person voted for as Vice-President, and of the number of votes for
each, which lists they shall sign and certify, and transmit sealed to the
seat of the Government of the United States, directed to the President
of the Senate; the President of the Senate shall, in the presence of the
Senate and House of Representatives, open all the certificates and the
votes shall then be counted; - The person having the greatest number
of votes for President, shall be the President, if such number be a
majority of the whole number of Electors appointed; and if no person
have such majority, then from the persons having the highest numbers
not exceeding three on the list of those voted for as President, the
House of Representatives shall choose immediately, by ballot, the
President. But in choosing the President, the votes shall be taken by
States, the representation from each State having one vote; a quorum
for this purpose shall consist of a member or members from two-
thirds of the States, and a majority of all the States shall be necessary to
a choice. And if the House of Representatives shall not choose a
President whenever the right of choice shall devolve upon them,
before the fourth day of March next following, then the Vice-President
shall act as President, as in case of the death or other constitutional
disability of the President.(The words in italics were superseded by
Amendment XX)

3. The person having the greatest number of votes as Vice-President,
shall be the Vice-President, if such numbers be a majority of the whole
number of electors appointed, and if no person have a majority, then
from the two highest numbers on the list, the Senate shall choose the
Vice-President; a quorum for the purpose shall consist of two-thirds of
the whole number of Senators, and a majority of the whole number

shall be necessary to a choice. But no person constitutionally ineligible
to the office of President shall be eligible to that of Vice-President of
the United States.

XIII - Slavery Abolished

Passed by Congress January 31, 1865. Ratified December 6, 1865.

1. Neither slavery nor involuntary servitude, except as a punishment
for crime whereof the party shall have been duly convicted, shall exist
within the United States, or any place subject to their jurisdiction.

2. Congress shall have power to enforce this article by appropriate
legislation.

XIV - Citizen rights not to be abridged

Passed by Congress June 13, 1866. Ratified July 9, 1868

1. All persons born or naturalized in the United States, and subject to
the jurisdiction thereof, are citizens of the United States and of the
State wherein they reside. No State shall make or enforce any law
which shall abridge the privileges or immunities of citizens of the
United States; nor shall any State deprive any person of life, liberty, or
property, without due process of law; nor to deny to any person within
its jurisdiction the equal protection of the laws.

2. Representatives shall be apportioned among the several States
according to their respective numbers, counting the whole number of
persons in each State, excluding Indians not taxed. But when the right
to vote at any election for the choice of Electors for President and
Vice-President of the United States, Representatives in Congress, the
executive and judicial officers of a State, or the members of the
legislature thereof, is denied to any of the male inhabitants of such
State, being twenty-one years of age, and citizens of the United States,
or in any way abridged, except for participation in rebellion, or other

crime, the basis of representation therein shall be reduced in the proportion which the number of such male citizens shall bear to the whole number of male citizens twenty-one years of age in such State.

3. No person shall be a Senator or Representative in Congress, or Elector of President and Vice-President, or hold any office, civil or military, under the United States, or under any State, who, having previously taken an oath, as a member of Congress, or as an officer of the United States, or as a member of any State Legislature, or as an executive or judicial officer of any State, to support the Constitution of the United States, shall have engaged in insurrection or rebellion against the same, or given aid or comfort to the enemies thereof. But Congress may by a vote of two-thirds of each House, remove such disability.

4. The validity of the public debt of the United States, authorized by law, including debts incurred for payment of pensions and bounties for services in suppressing insurrection or rebellion, shall not be questioned. But neither the United States nor any State shall assume or pay any debt or obligation incurred in aid of insurrection or rebellion against the United States, or any claim for the loss or emancipation of any slave; but all such debts, obligations and claims shall be held illegal and void.

5. The Congress shall have the power to enforce, by appropriate legislation, the provisions of this article.

XV - Race no bar to voting rights

Passed by Congress February 26, 1869. Ratified February 3, 1870.

1. The right of citizens of the United States to vote shall not be denied or abridged by the United States or by any State on account of race, color, or previous condition of servitude.

2. The Congress shall have the power to enforce this article by appropriate legislation.

XVI - Income taxes authorized

Passed by Congress July 2, 1909. Ratified February 3, 1913.

The Congress shall have power to lay and collect taxes on incomes, from whatever sources derived, without apportionment among the several States, and without regard to any census or enumeration.

XVII - U.S. Senators to be elected by direct popular vote

Passed by Congress May 13, 1912. Ratified April 8, 1913.

1. The Senate of the United States shall be composed of two Senators from each State, elected by the people thereof, for six years; and each Senator shall have one vote. The electors in each State shall have the qualifications requisite for electors of the most numerous branch of the State Legislatures.

2. When vacancies happen in the representation of any State in the Senate, the executive authority of such State shall issue writs of election to fill such vacancies: Provided, That the Legislature of any State may empower the Executive thereof to make temporary appointments until the people fill the vacancies by election as the Legislature may direct.

3. This amendment shall not be so construed as to affect the election or term of any Senator chosen before it becomes valid as part of the Constitution.

XVIII - Liquor Prohibition

Passed by Congress December 18, 1917. Ratified January 16, 1919.

Altered by Amendment XXI

1. After one year from the ratification of this article the manufacture, sale, or transportation of intoxicating liquors within, the importation thereof into, or the exportation thereof from the United States and all territory subject to the jurisdiction thereof for beverage purposes is hereby prohibited.

2. The Congress and the several States shall have concurrent power to enforce this article by appropriate legislation.

3. This article shall be inoperative unless it shall have been ratified as an amendment to the Constitution by the Legislatures of the several States, as provided in the Constitution, within seven years from the date of the submission hereof to the States by the Congress.

XIX - Giving nationwide suffrage to women

Passed by Congress June 4, 1919. Ratified August 18, 1920.

1. The right of citizens of the United States to vote shall not be denied or abridged by the United States or by any State on account of sex.

2. Congress shall have power to enforce this article by appropriate legislation.

XX - Terms of the President and Vice-President

This Amendment altered Article 1 Section 4 Part 2 and Article 2 Section 1 Part5

Passed by Congress March 2, 1932. Ratified January 23, 1933

1. The terms of the President and the Vice-President shall end at noon on the 20th day of January, and the terms of Senators and Representatives at noon on the 3rd day of January, of the years in

which such terms would have ended if this article had not been ratified; and the terms of their successors shall then begin.

2. The Congress shall assemble at least once in every year, and such meeting shall begin at noon on the 3rd day of January, unless they shall by law appoint a different day.

3. If, at the time fixed for the beginning of the term of the President, the President elect shall have died, the Vice-President elect shall become President. If a President shall not have been chosen before the time fixed for the beginning of his term, or if the President elect shall have failed to qualify, then the Vice-President elect shall act as President until a President shall have qualified; and the Congress may by law provide for the case wherein neither a President elect nor a Vice-President shall have qualified, declaring who shall then act as President, or the manner in which one who is to act shall be selected, and such person shall act accordingly until a President or Vice-President shall have qualified.

4. The Congress may by law provide for the case of the death of any of the persons from whom the House of representatives may choose a President whenever the right of choice shall have devolved upon them, and for the case of the death of any of the persons from whom the Senate may choose a Vice-President whenever the right of choice shall have devolved upon them.

5. Sections 1 and 2 shall take effect on the 15th day of October following the ratification of this article (October 1933).

6. This article shall be inoperative unless it shall have been ratified as an amendment to the Constitution by the Legislatures of three-fourths of the several States within seven years from the date of its submission.

XXI - Repeal of Amendment XVIII

Passed by Congress February 20, 1933. Ratified December 5, 1933.

1. The Eighteenth article of amendment to the Constitution of the United States is hereby repealed.

2. The transportation or importation into any State, Territory, or Possession of the United States for delivery or use therein of intoxicating liquors, in violation of the laws thereof, is hereby prohibited.

3. This article shall be inoperative unless it shall have been ratified as an amendment to the Constitution by conventions in the several States, as provided in the Constitution, within seven years from the date of the submission hereof to the States by the Congress.

XXII - Limiting presidential terms of office

Passed by Congress March 21, 1947. Ratified February 27, 1951.

1. No person shall be elected to the office of the President more than twice, and no person who has held the office of President, or acted as President, for more that two years of a term to which some other person was elected President shall be elected to the office of President more than once.

2. But this Article shall not apply to any person holding the office of President when this Article was proposed by Congress, and shall not prevent any person who may be holding the office of President, or acting as President, during the term the term within which this Article becomes operative from holding the office of President or acting as President during the remainder of such term.

3. This article shall be inoperative unless it shall have been ratified as an amendment to the Constitution by the Legislatures of three-fourths of the several States within seven years from the date of its submission to the States by the Congress.

XXIII - Presidential vote for the District of Columbia

Passed by Congress June 16, 1960. Ratified March 29, 1961.

1. The District constituting the seat of Government of the United States shall appoint in such manner as Congress may direct:

2. A number of electors of President and Vice President equal to the whole number of Senators and Representatives in Congress to which the District would be entitled if it were a State, but in no event more than the least populous State; they shall be in addition to those appointed by the States, but they shall be considered, for the purposes of the election of President and Vice President, to be electors appointed by a State; and they shall meet in the District and perform such duties as provided by the twelfth article of amendment.

3. The Congress shall have power to enforce this article by appropriate legislation.

XXIV - Barring poll tax in federal elections

This Amendment altered Article 1 Section 2 Part 3

Passed by Congress August 27, 1962. Ratified January 23,1964.

1. The right of citizens of the United States to vote in any primary or other election for President or Vice President, for electors for President or Vice President, or for Senator or Representative in Congress, shall not be denied or abridged by the United States or any State by reason of failure to pay poll tax or any other tax.

2. Congress shall have power to enforce this article by appropriate legislation.

XXV - Presidential disability and succession

This Amendment altered Article 2 Section 1 Part 5

Passed by Congress July 6, 1965. Ratified February 10, 1967.

1. In case of the removal of the President from office or of his death or resignation, the Vice President shall become President.

2. Whenever there is a vacancy in the office of the Vice President, the President shall nominate a Vice President who shall take the office upon confirmation by a majority vote of both houses of Congress

3. Whenever the President transmits to the President Pro tempore of the Senate and the Speaker of the House of Representatives his written declaration that he is unable to discharge the powers and duties of his office, and until he transmits to them a written declaration to the contrary, such powers and duties shall be discharged by the Vice President as Acting President.

4. Whenever the Vice President and a majority of either the principal officers of the executive departments or of such other body as Congress may by law provide, transmits to the President Pro tempore of the Senate and the Speaker of the House of Representatives their written declaration that the President is unable to discharge the powers and duties of his office, the Vice President shall immediately assume the powers and duties of the office as Acting President.

5. Thereafter, when the President transmits to the President Pro tempore of the Senate and the Speaker of the House of Representatives his written declaration that no inability exists, he shall resume the powers and duties of his office unless the Vice President and a majority of either the principal officers of the executive departments or of such other body as Congress may by law provide, transmits within four days to the President Pro tempore of the Senate and the Speaker of the House of Representatives their written declaration that the President is unable to discharge the powers and duties of his office. Thereupon Congress shall decide the issue,

assembling within forty-eight hours for that purpose if not in session. If the Congress, within twenty-one days after receipt of the latter written declaration, or, if Congress is not in session within twenty-one days after Congress is required to assemble, determines by two-thirds vote of both houses that the President is unable to discharge the powers and duties of his office, the Vice President shall continue to discharge the same as Acting President; otherwise, the President shall resume the powers and duties of his office.

XXVI - Lowering the voting age to 18 years

This Amendment altered Article 1 Section 9 Part 4

Passed by Congress March 23, 1971. Ratified June 30, 1971.

The right of citizens of the United States, who are 18 years of age or older, to vote shall not be denied or abridged by the United States or any state on account of age.

The Congress shall have power to enforce this article by appropriate legislation.

XXVII - Congressional Pay

This Amendment altered Article 1 Section 3 Part 1 and Article 1 Section 3 Part 2

Passed by Congress September 25, 1789. Ratified May 7, 1992.

No law, varying the compensation for services of the Senators and Representatives, shall take effect, until an election of Representatives shall have intervened.

The Unanimous Declaration of Independence made by the Delegates of the People of Texas in General Convention at the town of Washington on the 2nd day of March 1836.

When a government has ceased to protect the lives, liberty and property of the people, from whom its legitimate powers are derived, and for the advancement of whose happiness it was instituted, and so far from being a guarantee for the enjoyment of those inestimable and inalienable rights, becomes an instrument in the hands of evil rulers for their oppression.

When the Federal Republican Constitution of their country, which they have sworn to support, no longer has a substantial existence, and the whole nature of their government has been forcibly changed, without their consent, from a restricted federative republic, composed of sovereign states, to a consolidated central military despotism, in which every interest is disregarded but that of the army and the priesthood, both the eternal enemies of civil liberty, the everready minions of power, and the usual instruments of tyrants.

When, long after the spirit of the constitution has departed, moderation is at length so far lost by those in power, that even the semblance of freedom is removed, and the forms themselves of the constitution discontinued, and so far from their petitions and remonstrances being regarded, the agents who bear them are thrown into dungeons, and mercenary armies sent forth to force a new government upon them at the point of the bayonet.

When, in consequence of such acts of malfeasance and abdication on the part of the government, anarchy prevails, and civil society is dissolved into its original elements. In such a crisis, the first law of nature, the right of self-preservation, the inherent and inalienable rights of the people to appeal to first principles, and take their political affairs into their own hands in extreme cases, enjoins it as a right towards themselves, and a sacred obligation to their posterity, to abolish such government, and create another in its stead, calculated to rescue them from impending dangers, and to secure their future welfare and happiness.

Nations, as well as individuals, are amenable for their acts to the public opinion of mankind. A statement of a part of our grievances is therefore submitted to an impartial world, in justification of the hazardous but unavoidable step now taken, of severing our political connection with the Mexican people, and assuming an independent attitude among the nations of the earth.

The Mexican government, by its colonization laws, invited and induced the Anglo-American population of Texas to colonize its wilderness under the pledged faith of a written constitution, that they should continue to enjoy that constitutional liberty and republican government to which they had been habituated in the land of their birth, the United States of America.

In this expectation they have been cruelly disappointed, inasmuch as the Mexican nation has acquiesced in the late changes made in the government by General Antonio Lopez de Santa Anna, who having overturned the constitution of his country, now offers us the cruel alternative, either to abandon our homes, acquired by so many privations, or submit to the most intolerable of all tyranny, the combined despotism of the sword and the priesthood.

It has sacrificed our welfare to the state of Coahuila, by which our interests have been continually depressed through a jealous and partial course of legislation, carried on at a far distant seat of government, by a hostile majority, in an unknown tongue, and this too, notwithstanding we have petitioned in the humblest terms for the establishment of a separate state government, and have, in accordance with the provisions of the national constitution, presented to the general Congress a republican constitution, which was, without just cause, contemptuously rejected.

It incarcerated in a dungeon, for a long time, one of our citizens, for no other cause but a zealous endeavor to procure the acceptance of our constitution, and the establishment of a state government.

It has failed and refused to secure, on a firm basis, the right of trial by jury, that palladium of civil liberty, and only safe guarantee for the life, liberty, and property of the citizen.

It has failed to establish any public system of education, although possessed of almost boundless resources, (the public domain,) and although it is an axiom in political science, that unless a people are educated and enlightened, it is idle to expect the continuance of civil liberty, or the capacity for self government.

It has suffered the military commandants, stationed among us, to exercise arbitrary acts of oppression and tyrany, thus trampling upon the most sacred rights of the citizens, and rendering the military superior to the civil power.

It has dissolved, by force of arms, the state Congress of Coahuila and Texas, and obliged our representatives to fly for their lives from the seat of government, thus depriving us of the fundamental political right of representation.

It has demanded the surrender of a number of our citizens, and ordered military detachments to seize and carry them into the Interior for trial, in contempt of the civil authorities, and in defiance of the laws and the constitution.

It has made piratical attacks upon our commerce, by commissioning foreign desperadoes, and authorizing them to seize our vessels, and convey the property of our citizens to far distant ports for confiscation.

It denies us the right of worshipping the Almighty according to the dictates of our own conscience, by the support of a national religion, calculated to promote the temporal interest of its human functionaries, rather than the glory of the true and living God.

It has demanded us to deliver up our arms, which are essential to our defence, the rightful property of freemen, and formidable only to tyrannical governments.

It has invaded our country both by sea and by land, with intent to lay waste our territory, and drive us from our homes; and has now a large mercenary army advancing, to carry on against us a war of extermination.

It has, through its emissaries, incited the merciless savage, with the tomahawk and scalping knife, to massacre the inhabitants of our defenseless frontiers.

It hath been, during the whole time of our connection with it, the contemptible sport and victim of successive military revolutions, and hath continually exhibited every characteristic of a weak, corrupt, and tyrranical government.

These, and other grievances, were patiently borne by the people of Texas, untill they reached that point at which forbearance ceases to be a virtue. We then took up arms in defence of the national constitution. We appealed to our Mexican brethren for assistance. Our appeal has been made in vain. Though months have elapsed, no sympathetic response has yet been heard from the Interior. We are, therefore, forced to the melancholy conclusion, that the Mexican people have acquiesced in the destruction of their liberty, and the substitution therfor of a military government; that they are unfit to be free, and incapable of self government.

The necessity of self-preservation, therefore, now decrees our eternal political separation.

We, therefore, the delegates with plenary powers of the people of
Texas, in solemn convention assembled, appealing to a candid world
for the necessities of our condition, do hereby resolve and declare, that
our political connection with the Mexican nation has forever ended,
and that the people of Texas do now constitute a free, Sovereign, and
independent republic, and are fully invested with all the rights and
attributes which properly belong to independent nations; and,
conscious of the rectitude of our intentions, we fearlessly and
confidently commit the issue to the decision of the Supreme arbiter of
the destinies of nations.

Richard Ellis, President of the Convention and Delegate from Red
River.

Charles B. Stewart
Tho. Barnett
John S. D. Byrom
Francis Ruis
J. Antonio Navarro
Jesse B. Badgett
Wm D. Lacy
William Menifee
Jn. Fisher
Matthew Caldwell
William Motley
Lorenzo de Zavala
Stephen H. Everett
George W. Smyth
Elijah Stapp
Claiborne West
Wm. B. Scates
M. B. Menard
A. B. Hardin
J. W. Burton
Thos. J. Gazley

R. M. Coleman
Sterling C. Robertson
James Collinsworth
Edwin Waller
Asa Brigham
Geo. C. Childress
Bailey Hardeman
Rob. Potter
Thomas Jefferson Rusk
Chas. S. Taylor
John S. Roberts
Robert Hamilton
Collin McKinney
Albert H. Latimer
James Power
Sam Houston
David Thomas
Edwd. Conrad
Martin Palmer
Edwin O. Legrand
Stephen W. Blount
Jms. Gaines
Wm. Clark, Jr.
Sydney O. Pennington
Wm. Carrol Crawford
Jno. Turner
Benj. Briggs Goodrich
G. W. Barnett
James G. Swisher
Jesse Grimes
S. Rhoads Fisher
John W. Moore
John W. Bower
Saml. A. Maverick (from Bejar)
Sam P. Carson
A. Briscoe

J. B. Woods
H. S. Kimble, Secretary

Declaration of the Immediate Causes Which Induce and Justify the Secession of South Carolina from the Federal Union: December 24, 1860

The people of the State of South Carolina, in Convention assembled, on the 26th day of April, A.D., 1852, declared that the frequent violations of the Constitution of the United States, by the Federal Government, and its encroachments upon the reserved rights of the States, fully justified this State in then withdrawing from the Federal Union; but in deference to the opinions and wishes of the other slaveholding States, she forbore at that time to exercise this right. Since that time, these encroachments have continued to increase, and further forbearance ceases to be a virtue.

And now the State of South Carolina having resumed her separate and equal place among nations, deems it due to herself, to the remaining United States of America, and to the nations of the world, that she should declare the immediate causes which have led to this act.

In the year 1765, that portion of the British Empire embracing Great Britain, undertook to make laws for the government of that portion composed of the thirteen American Colonies. A struggle for the right of self-government ensued, which resulted, on the 4th of July, 1776, in a Declaration, by the Colonies, "that they are, and of right ought to be, FREE AND INDEPENDENT STATES; and that, as free and independent States, they have full power to levy war, conclude peace, contract alliances, establish commerce, and to do all other acts and things which independent States may of right do."

They further solemnly declared that whenever any "form of government becomes destructive of the ends for which it was established, it is the right of the people to alter or abolish it, and to institute a new government." Deeming the Government of Great Britain to have become destructive of these ends, they declared that the Colonies "are absolved from all allegiance to the British Crown, and that all political connection between them and the State of Great Britain is, and ought to be, totally dissolved."

In pursuance of this Declaration of Independence, each of the thirteen States proceeded to exercise its separate sovereignty; adopted for itself a Constitution, and appointed officers for the administration of government in all its departments-- Legislative, Executive and Judicial. For purposes of defense, they united their arms and their counsels; and, in 1778, they entered into a League known as the Articles of Confederation, whereby they agreed to entrust the administration of their external relations to a common agent, known as the Congress of the United States, expressly declaring, in the first Article "that each State retains its sovereignty, freedom and independence, and every power, jurisdiction and right which is not, by this Confederation, expressly delegated to the United States in Congress assembled."

Under this Confederation the war of the Revolution was carried on, and on the 3rd of September, 1783, the contest ended, and a definite Treaty was signed by Great Britain, in which she acknowledged the independence of the Colonies in the following terms: "ARTICLE 1-- His Britannic Majesty acknowledges the said United States, viz: New Hampshire, Massachusetts Bay, Rhode Island and Providence Plantations, Connecticut, New York, New Jersey, Pennsylvania, Delaware, Maryland, Virginia, North Carolina, South Carolina and Georgia, to be FREE, SOVEREIGN AND INDEPENDENT STATES; that he treats with them as such; and for himself, his heirs and successors, relinquishes all claims to the government, propriety and territorial rights of the same and every part thereof."

Thus were established the two great principles asserted by the Colonies, namely: the right of a State to govern itself; and the right of a people to abolish a Government when it becomes destructive of the ends for which it was instituted. And concurrent with the establishment of these principles, was the fact, that each Colony became and was recognized by the mother Country a FREE, SOVEREIGN AND INDEPENDENT STATE.

In 1787, Deputies were appointed by the States to revise the Articles of Confederation, and on 17th September, 1787, these Deputies recommended for the adoption of the States, the Articles of Union, known as the Constitution of the United States.

The parties to whom this Constitution was submitted, were the several sovereign States; they were to agree or disagree, and when nine of them agreed the compact was to take effect among those concurring; and the General Government, as the common agent, was then invested with their authority.

If only nine of the thirteen States had concurred, the other four would have remained as they then were-- separate, sovereign States, independent of any of the provisions of the Constitution. In fact, two of the States did not accede to the Constitution until long after it had gone into operation among the other eleven; and during that interval, they each exercised the functions of an independent nation.

By this Constitution, certain duties were imposed upon the several States, and the exercise of certain of their powers was restrained, which necessarily implied their continued existence as sovereign States. But to remove all doubt, an amendment was added, which declared that the powers not delegated to the United States by the Constitution, nor prohibited by it to the States, are reserved to the States, respectively, or to the people. On the 23d May , 1788, South Carolina, by a Convention of her People, passed an Ordinance assenting to this Constitution, and afterwards altered her own Constitution, to conform herself to the obligations she had undertaken.

Thus was established, by compact between the States, a Government with definite objects and powers, limited to the express words of the grant. This limitation left the whole remaining mass of power subject to the clause reserving it to the States or to the people, and rendered unnecessary any specification of reserved rights.

We hold that the Government thus established is subject to the two great principles asserted in the Declaration of Independence; and we hold further, that the mode of its formation subjects it to a third fundamental principle, namely: the law of compact. We maintain that in every compact between two or more parties, the obligation is mutual; that the failure of one of the contracting parties to perform a material part of the agreement, entirely releases the obligation of the other; and that where no arbiter is provided, each party is remitted to his own judgment to determine the fact of failure, with all its consequences.

In the present case, that fact is established with certainty. We assert that fourteen of the States have deliberately refused, for years past, to fulfill their constitutional obligations, and we refer to their own Statutes for the proof.

The Constitution of the United States, in its fourth Article, provides as follows: "No person held to service or labor in one State, under the laws thereof, escaping into another, shall, in consequence of any law or regulation therein, be discharged from such service or labor, but shall be delivered up, on claim of the party to whom such service or labor may be due."

This stipulation was so material to the compact, that without it that compact would not have been made. The greater number of the contracting parties held slaves, and they had previously evinced their estimate of the value of such a stipulation by making it a condition in the Ordinance for the government of the territory ceded by Virginia, which now composes the States north of the Ohio River.

The same article of the Constitution stipulates also for rendition by the several States of fugitives from justice from the other States.

The General Government, as the common agent, passed laws to carry into effect these stipulations of the States. For many years these laws were executed. But an increasing hostility on the part of the non-

slaveholding States to the institution of slavery, has led to a disregard
of their obligations, and the laws of the General Government have
ceased to effect the objects of the Constitution. The States of Maine,
New Hampshire, Vermont, Massachusetts, Connecticut, Rhode Island,
New York, Pennsylvania, Illinois, Indiana, Michigan, Wisconsin and
Iowa, have enacted laws which either nullify the Acts of Congress or
render useless any attempt to execute them. In many of these States
the fugitive is discharged from service or labor claimed, and in none of
them has the State Government complied with the stipulation made in
the Constitution. The State of New Jersey, at an early day, passed a law
in conformity with her constitutional obligation; but the current of
anti-slavery feeling has led her more recently to enact laws which
render inoperative the remedies provided by her own law and by the
laws of Congress. In the State of New York even the right of transit
for a slave has been denied by her tribunals; and the States of Ohio and
Iowa have refused to surrender to justice fugitives charged with
murder, and with inciting servile insurrection in the State of Virginia.
Thus the constituted compact has been deliberately broken and
disregarded by the non-slaveholding States, and the consequence
follows that South Carolina is released from her obligation.

The ends for which the Constitution was framed are declared by itself
to be "to form a more perfect union, establish justice, insure domestic
tranquility, provide for the common defence, promote the general
welfare, and secure the blessings of liberty to ourselves and our
posterity."

These ends it endeavored to accomplish by a Federal Government, in
which each State was recognized as an equal, and had separate control
over its own institutions. The right of property in slaves was
recognized by giving to free persons distinct political rights, by giving
them the right to represent, and burthening them with direct taxes for
three-fifths of their slaves; by authorizing the importation of slaves for
twenty years; and by stipulating for the rendition of fugitives from
labor.

We affirm that these ends for which this Government was instituted have been defeated, and the Government itself has been made destructive of them by the action of the non-slaveholding States. Those States have assume the right of deciding upon the propriety of our domestic institutions; and have denied the rights of property established in fifteen of the States and recognized by the Constitution; they have denounced as sinful the institution of slavery; they have permitted open establishment among them of societies, whose avowed object is to disturb the peace and to eloign the property of the citizens of other States. They have encouraged and assisted thousands of our slaves to leave their homes; and those who remain, have been incited by emissaries, books and pictures to servile insurrection.

For twenty-five years this agitation has been steadily increasing, until it has now secured to its aid the power of the common Government. Observing the forms of the Constitution, a sectional party has found within that Article establishing the Executive Department, the means of subverting the Constitution itself. A geographical line has been drawn across the Union, and all the States north of that line have united in the election of a man to the high office of President of the United States, whose opinions and purposes are hostile to slavery. He is to be entrusted with the administration of the common Government, because he has declared that that "Government cannot endure permanently half slave, half free," and that the public mind must rest in the belief that slavery is in the course of ultimate extinction.

This sectional combination for the submersion of the Constitution, has been aided in some of the States by elevating to citizenship, persons who, by the supreme law of the land, are incapable of becoming citizens; and their votes have been used to inaugurate a new policy, hostile to the South, and destructive of its beliefs and safety.

On the 4th day of March next, this party will take possession of the Government. It has announced that the South shall be excluded from the common territory, that the judicial tribunals shall be made sectional, and that a war must be waged against slavery until it shall cease throughout the United States.

The guaranties of the Constitution will then no longer exist; the equal rights of the States will be lost. The slaveholding States will no longer have the power of self-government, or self-protection, and the Federal Government will have become their enemy.

Sectional interest and animosity will deepen the irritation, and all hope of remedy is rendered vain, by the fact that public opinion at the North has invested a great political error with the sanction of more erroneous religious belief.

We, therefore, the People of South Carolina, by our delegates in Convention assembled, appealing to the Supreme Judge of the world for the rectitude of our intentions, have solemnly declared that the Union heretofore existing between this State and the other States of North America, is dissolved, and that the State of South Carolina has resumed her position among the nations of the world, as a separate and independent State; with full power to levy war, conclude peace, contract alliances, establish commerce, and to do all other acts and things which independent States may of right do.

Adopted December 24, 1860

The people of Georgia having dissolved their political connection with the Government of the United States of America, present to their confederates and the world the causes which have led to the separation. For the last ten years we have had numerous and serious causes of complaint against our non-slave-holding confederate States with reference to the subject of African slavery. They have endeavored to weaken our security, to disturb our domestic peace and tranquility, and persistently refused to comply with their express constitutional obligations to us in reference to that property, and by the use of their power in the Federal Government have striven to deprive us of an equal enjoyment of the common Territories of the Republic. This hostile policy of our confederates has been pursued with every circumstance of aggravation which could arouse the passions and excite the hatred of our people, and has placed the two sections of the Union for many years past in the condition of virtual civil war. Our people, still attached to the Union from habit and national traditions, and averse to change, hoped that time, reason, and argument would bring, if not redress, at least exemption from further insults, injuries, and dangers. Recent events have fully dissipated all such hopes and demonstrated the necessity of separation. Our Northern confederates, after a full and calm hearing of all the facts, after a fair warning of our purpose not to submit to the rule of the authors of all these wrongs and injuries, have by a large majority committed the Government of the United States into their hands. The people of Georgia, after an equally full and fair and deliberate hearing of the case, have declared with equal firmness that they shall not rule over them. A brief history of the rise, progress, and policy of anti-slavery and the political organization into whose hands the administration of the Federal Government has been committed will fully justify the pronounced verdict of the people of Georgia. The party of Lincoln, called the Republican party, under its present name and organization, is of recent origin. It is admitted to be an anti-slavery party. While it attracts to itself by its creed the scattered advocates of exploded political heresies, of condemned theories in political economy, the advocates of commercial restrictions, of protection, of special privileges, of waste and corruption in the administration of Government, anti-slavery is its mission and its purpose. By anti-slavery it is made a power in the state. The question of slavery was the great difficulty in the way of the formation of the Constitution. While the subordination and the political and social inequality of the African race was fully conceded by all, it was plainly apparent that slavery would soon disappear from what are now the non-slave-holding States of the original thirteen. The opposition to slavery was then, as now, general in those States and the Constitution was made with direct reference to that fact. But a distinct abolition party was not formed in the United States for more than half a century after the Government went into operation. The main reason was that the North, even if united, could not control both branches of the Legislature during any portion of that time. Therefore such an organization must have resulted either in utter failure or in the total overthrow of the Government. The material prosperity of the North was greatly dependent on the Federal Government; that of the the South not at all. In the first years of the Republic the navigating, commercial, and manufacturing interests of the North began to seek profit and aggrandizement at the expense of the agricultural interests. Even the owners of fishing smacks sought and obtained bounties for pursuing their own business (which yet continue), and $500,000 is now paid them annually out of the Treasury. The navigating interests begged for protection against foreign shipbuilders and against competition in the coasting trade. Congress granted both requests, and by prohibitory acts gave an absolute monopoly of this business to each of their interests, which they enjoy without diminution to this day. Not content with these great and unjust advantages, they have sought to throw the legitimate burden of their business as much as possible upon the public; they have succeeded in throwing the cost of light-houses, buoys, and the maintenance of their seamen upon the Treasury, and the Government now pays above $2,000,000 annually for the support of these objects. Theses interests, in connection with the commercial and manufacturing classes, have also succeeded, by means of subventions to mail steamers and the reduction in postage, in relieving their business from the payment of about $7,000,000 annually, throwing it upon the public Treasury under the name of postal deficiency. The manufacturing interests entered into the same struggle early, and has clamored steadily for Government bounties and special favors. This interest was confined mainly to the Eastern and Middle non-slave-holding States. Wielding these great States it held great power and influence, and its demands were in full proportion to its power. The manufacturers and miners wisely based their demands upon special facts and reasons rather than upon general principles, and thereby mollified much of the opposition of the opposing interest. They pleaded in their favor the infancy of their business in this country, the scarcity of labor and capital, the hostile legislation of other countries toward them, the great necessity of their fabrics in the time of war, and the necessity of high duties to pay the debt incurred in our war for independence. These reasons prevailed, and they received for many years enormous bounties by the general acquiescence of the whole country.

But when these reasons ceased they were no less clamorous for Government protection, but their clamors were less heeded-- the country had put the principle of protection upon trial and condemned it. After having enjoyed protection to the extent of from 15 to 200 per cent. upon their entire business for above thirty years, the act of 1846 was passed. It avoided sudden change, but the principle was settled, and free trade, low duties, and economy in public expenditures was the verdict of the American people. The South and the Northwestern States sustained this policy. There was but small hope of its reversal; upon the direct issue, none at all.

All these classes saw this and felt it and cast about for new allies. The anti-slavery sentiment of the North offered the best chance for success. An anti-slavery party must necessarily look to the North alone for support, but a united North was now strong enough to control the Government in all of its departments, and a sectional party was therefore determined upon. Time and issues upon slavery were necessary to its completion and final triumph. The feeling of anti-slavery, which it was well known was very general among the people of

the North, had been long dormant or passive; it needed only a
question to arouse it into aggressive activity. This question was before
us. We had acquired a large territory by successful war with Mexico;
Congress had to govern it; how, in relation to slavery, was the question
then demanding solution. This state of facts gave form and shape to
the anti-slavery sentiment throughout the North and the conflict
began. Northern anti-slavery men of all parties asserted the right to
exclude slavery from the territory by Congressional legislation and
demanded the prompt and efficient exercise of this power to that end.
This insulting and unconstitutional demand was met with great
moderation and firmness by the South. We had shed our blood and
paid our money for its acquisition; we demanded a division of it on the
line of the Missouri restriction or an equal participation in the whole of
it. These propositions were refused, the agitation became general, and
the public danger was great. The case of the South was impregnable.
The price of the acquisition was the blood and treasure of both
sections-- of all, and, therefore, it belonged to all upon the principles of
equity and justice.

The Constitution delegated no power to Congress to excluded either
party from its free enjoyment; therefore our right was good under the
Constitution. Our rights were further fortified by the practice of the
Government from the beginning. Slavery was forbidden in the country
northwest of the Ohio River by what is called the ordinance of 1787.
That ordinance was adopted under the old confederation and by the
assent of Virginia, who owned and ceded the country, and therefore
this case must stand on its own special circumstances. The
Government of the United States claimed territory by virtue of the
treaty of 1783 with Great Britain, acquired territory by cession from
Georgia and North Carolina, by treaty from France, and by treaty from
Spain. These acquisitions largely exceeded the original limits of the
Republic. In all of these acquisitions the policy of the Government was
uniform. It opened them to the settlement of all the citizens of all the
States of the Union. They emigrated thither with their property of
every kind (including slaves). All were equally protected by public
authority in their persons and property until the inhabitants became

sufficiently numerous and otherwise capable of bearing the burdens and performing the duties of self-government, when they were admitted into the Union upon equal terms with the other States, with whatever republican constitution they might adopt for themselves.

Under this equally just and beneficent policy law and order, stability and progress, peace and prosperity marked every step of the progress of these new communities until they entered as great and prosperous commonwealths into the sisterhood of American States. In 1820 the North endeavored to overturn this wise and successful policy and demanded that the State of Missouri should not be admitted into the Union unless she first prohibited slavery within her limits by her constitution. After a bitter and protracted struggle the North was defeated in her special object, but her policy and position led to the adoption of a section in the law for the admission of Missouri, prohibiting slavery in all that portion of the territory acquired from France lying North of 36 [degrees] 30 [minutes] north latitude and outside of Missouri. The venerable Madison at the time of its adoption declared it unconstitutional. Mr. Jefferson condemned the restriction and foresaw its consequences and predicted that it would result in the dissolution of the Union. His prediction is now history. The North demanded the application of the principle of prohibition of slavery to all of the territory acquired from Mexico and all other parts of the public domain then and in all future time. It was the announcement of her purpose to appropriate to herself all the public domain then owned and thereafter to be acquired by the United States. The claim itself was less arrogant and insulting than the reason with which she supported it. That reason was her fixed purpose to limit, restrain, and finally abolish slavery in the States where it exists. The South with great unanimity declared her purpose to resist the principle of prohibition to the last extremity. This particular question, in connection with a series of questions affecting the same subject, was finally disposed of by the defeat of prohibitory legislation.

The Presidential election of 1852 resulted in the total overthrow of the advocates of restriction and their party friends. Immediately after this result the anti-slavery portion of the defeated party resolved to unite all the elements in the North opposed to slavery an to stake their future political fortunes upon their hostility to slavery everywhere. This is the party two whom the people of the North have committed the Government. They raised their standard in 1856 and were barely defeated. They entered the Presidential contest again in 1860 and succeeded.

The prohibition of slavery in the Territories, hostility to it everywhere, the equality of the black and white races, disregard of all constitutional guarantees it its favor, were boldly proclaimed by its leaders and applauded by its followers.

With these principles on their banners and these utterances on their lips the majority of the people of the North demand that we shall receive them as our rulers.

The prohibition of slavery in the Territories is the cardinal principle of this organization.

For forty years this question has been considered and debated in the halls of Congress, before the people, by the press, and before the tribunals of justice. The majority of the people of the North in 1860 decided it in their own favor. We refuse to submit to that judgment, and in vindication of our refusal we offer the Constitution of our country and point to the total absence of any express power to exclude us. We offer the practice of our Government for the first thirty years of its existence in complete refutation of the position that any such power is either necessary or proper to the execution of any other power in relation to the Territories. We offer the judgment of a large minority of the people of the North, amounting to more than one-third, who united with the unanimous voice of the South against this usurpation; and, finally, we offer the judgment of the Supreme Court of the United States, the highest judicial tribunal of our country, in our favor. This evidence ought to be conclusive that we have never surrendered this right. The conduct of our adversaries admonishes us that if we had surrendered it, it is time to resume it.

The faithless conduct of our adversaries is not confined to such acts as might aggrandize themselves or their section of the Union. They are content if they can only injure us. The Constitution declares that persons charged with crimes in one State and fleeing to another shall be delivered up on the demand of the executive authority of the State from which they may flee, to be tried in the jurisdiction where the crime was committed. It would appear difficult to employ language freer from ambiguity, yet for above twenty years the non-slave-holding States generally have wholly refused to deliver up to us persons charged with crimes affecting slave property. Our confederates, with punic faith, shield and give sanctuary to all criminals who seek to deprive us of this property or who use it to destroy us. This clause of the Constitution has no other sanction than their good faith; that is withheld from us; we are remediless in the Union; out of it we are remitted to the laws of nations.

A similar provision of the Constitution requires them to surrender fugitives from labor. This provision and the one last referred to were our main inducements for confederating with the Northern States. Without them it is historically true that we would have rejected the Constitution. In the fourth year of the Republic Congress passed a law to give full vigor and efficiency to this important provision. This act depended to a considerable degree upon the local magistrates in the several States for its efficiency. The non-slave-holding States generally repealed all laws intended to aid the execution of that act, and imposed penalties upon those citizens whose loyalty to the Constitution and their oaths might induce them to discharge their duty. Congress then passed the act of 1850, providing for the complete execution of this duty by Federal officers. This law, which their own bad faith rendered absolutely indispensible for the protection of constitutional rights, was instantly met with ferocious revilings and all conceivable modes of hostility. The Supreme Court unanimously, and their own local courts with equal unanimity (with the single and temporary exception of the supreme court of Wisconsin), sustained its constitutionality in all of its provisions. Yet it stands to-day a dead letter for all practicable purposes in every non-slave-holding State in the Union. We have their convenants, we have their oaths to keep and observe it, but the unfortunate claimant, even accompanied by a Federal officer with the mandate of the highest judicial authority in his hands, is everywhere met with fraud, with force, and with legislative enactments to elude, to resist, and defeat him. Claimants are murdered with impunity; officers of the law are beaten by frantic mobs instigated by inflammatory appeals from persons holding the highest public employment in these States, and supported by legislation in conflict with the clearest provisions of the Constitution, and even the ordinary principles of humanity. In several of our confederate States a citizen cannot travel the highway with his servant who may voluntarily accompany him, without being declared by law a felon and being subjected to infamous punishments. It is difficult to perceive how we could suffer more by the hostility than by the fraternity of such brethren.

The public law of civilized nations requires every State to restrain its citizens or subjects from committing acts injurious to the peace and security of any other State and from attempting to excite insurrection, or to lessen the security, or to disturb the tranquillity of their neighbors, and our Constitution wisely gives Congress the power to punish all offenses against the laws of nations.

These are sound and just principles which have received the approbation of just men in all countries and all centuries; but they are wholly disregarded by the people of the Northern States, and the Federal Government is impotent to maintain them. For twenty years past the abolitionists and their allies in the Northern States have been engaged in constant efforts to subvert our institutions and to excite insurrection and servile war among us. They have sent emissaries among us for the accomplishment of these purposes. Some of these efforts have received the public sanction of a majority of the leading men of the Republican party in the national councils, the same men who are now proposed as our rulers. These efforts have in one instance led to the actual invasion of one of the slave-holding States, and those of the murderers and incendiaries who escaped public justice by flight have found fraternal protection among our Northern confederates.

These are the same men who say the Union shall be preserved.

Such are the opinions and such are the practices of the Republican party, who have been called by their own votes to administer the Federal Government under the Constitution of the United States. We know their treachery; we know the shallow pretenses under which they daily disregard its plainest obligations. If we submit to them it will be our fault and not theirs. The people of Georgia have ever been willing to stand by this bargain, this contract; they have never sought to evade any of its obligations; they have never hitherto sought to establish any new government; they have struggled to maintain the ancient right of themselves and the human race through and by that Constitution. But they know the value of parchment rights in treacherous hands, and therefore they refuse to commit their own to the rulers whom the North offers us. Why? Because by their declared principles and policy they have outlawed $3,000,000,000 of our property in the common territories of the Union; put it under the ban of the Republic in the States where it exists and out of the protection of Federal law everywhere; because they give sanctuary to thieves and incendiaries who assail it to the whole extent of their power, in spite of their most solemn obligations and covenants; because their avowed purpose is to subvert our society and subject us not only to the loss of our property but the destruction of ourselves, our wives, and our children, and the desolation of our homes, our altars, and our firesides. To avoid these evils we resume the powers which our fathers delegated to the Government of the United States, and henceforth will seek new safeguards for our liberty, equality, security, and tranquillity.

[Approved, Tuesday, January 29, 1861]

A Declaration of the Causes which Impel the State of Texas to Secede
from the Federal Union: February 2, 1861

The government of the United States, by certain joint resolutions, bearing date the 1st day of March, in the year A.D. 1845, proposed to the Republic of Texas, then a free, sovereign and independent nation, the annexation of the latter to the former, as one of the co-equal states thereof,

The people of Texas, by deputies in convention assembled, on the fourth day of July of the same year, assented to and accepted said proposals and formed a constitution for the proposed State, upon which on the 29th day of December in the same year, said State was formally admitted into the Confederated Union.

Texas abandoned her separate national existence and consented to become one of the Confederated Union to promote her welfare, insure domestic tranquility and secure more substantially the blessings of peace and liberty to her people. She was received into the confederacy with her own constitution, under the guarantee of the federal constitution and the compact of annexation, that she should enjoy these blessings. She was received as a commonwealth holding, maintaining and protecting the institution known as negro slavery-- the servitude of the African to the white race within her limits-- a relation that had existed from the first settlement of her wilderness by the white race, and which her people intended should exist in all future time. Her institutions and geographical position established the strongest ties between her and other slave-holding States of the confederacy. Those ties have been strengthened by association. But what has been the course of the government of the United States, and of the people and authorities of the non-slave-holding States, since our connection with them?

The controlling majority of the Federal Government, under various pretences and disguises, has so administered the same as to exclude the citizens of the Southern States, unless under odious and unconstitutional restrictions, from all the immense territory owned in common by all the States on the Pacific Ocean, for the avowed purpose of acquiring sufficient power in the common government to use it as a means of destroying the institutions of Texas and her sister slaveholding States.

By the disloyalty of the Northern States and their citizens and the imbecility of the Federal Government, infamous combinations of incendiaries and outlaws have been permitted in those States and the common territory of Kansas to trample upon the federal laws, to war upon the lives and property of Southern citizens in that territory, and finally, by violence and mob law, to usurp the possession of the same as exclusively the property of the Northern States.

The Federal Government, while but partially under the control of these our unnatural and sectional enemies, has for years almost entirely failed to protect the lives and property of the people of Texas against the Indian savages on our border, and more recently against the murderous forays of banditti from the neighboring territory of Mexico; and when our State government has expended large amounts for such purpose, the Federal Government has refuse reimbursement therefor, thus rendering our condition more insecure and harassing than it was during the existence of the Republic of Texas.

These and other wrongs we have patiently borne in the vain hope that a returning sense of justice and humanity would induce a different course of administration.

When we advert to the course of individual non-slave-holding States, and that a majority of their citizens, our grievances assume far greater magnitude.

The States of Maine, Vermont, New Hampshire, Connecticut, Rhode Island, Massachusetts, New York, Pennsylvania, Ohio, Wisconsin, Michigan and Iowa, by solemn legislative enactments, have deliberately, directly or indirectly violated the 3rd clause of the 2nd section of the 4th article [the fugitive slave clause] of the federal constitution, and laws passed in pursuance thereof; thereby annulling a material provision of the compact, designed by its framers to perpetuate the amity between the members of the confederacy and to secure the rights of the slave-holding States in their domestic institutions-- a provision founded in justice and wisdom, and without the enforcement of which the compact fails to accomplish the object of its creation. Some of those States have imposed high fines and degrading penalties upon any of their citizens or officers who may carry out in good faith that provision of the compact, or the federal laws enacted in accordance therewith.

In all the non-slave-holding States, in violation of that good faith and comity which should exist between entirely distinct nations, the people have formed themselves into a great sectional party, now strong enough in numbers to control the affairs of each of those States, based upon an unnatural feeling of hostility to these Southern States and their beneficent and patriarchal system of African slavery, proclaiming the debasing doctrine of equality of all men, irrespective of race or color-- a doctrine at war with nature, in opposition to the experience of mankind, and in violation of the plainest revelations of Divine Law. They demand the abolition of negro slavery throughout the confederacy, the recognition of political equality between the white and negro races, and avow their determination to press on their crusade against us, so long as a negro slave remains in these States.

For years past this abolition organization has been actively sowing the seeds of discord through the Union, and has rendered the federal congress the arena for spreading firebrands and hatred between the slave-holding and non-slave-holding States.

By consolidating their strength, they have placed the slave-holding States in a hopeless minority in the federal congress, and rendered representation of no avail in protecting Southern rights against their exactions and encroachments.

They have proclaimed, and at the ballot box sustained, the revolutionary doctrine that there is a 'higher law' than the constitution and laws of our Federal Union, and virtually that they will disregard their oaths and trample upon our rights.

They have for years past encouraged and sustained lawless organizations to steal our slaves and prevent their recapture, and have repeatedly murdered Southern citizens while lawfully seeking their rendition.

They have invaded Southern soil and murdered unoffending citizens, and through the press their leading men and a fanatical pulpit have bestowed praise upon the actors and assassins in these crimes, while the governors of several of their States have refused to deliver parties implicated and indicted for participation in such offenses, upon the legal demands of the States aggrieved.

They have, through the mails and hired emissaries, sent seditious pamphlets and papers among us to stir up servile insurrection and bring blood and carnage to our firesides.

They have sent hired emissaries among us to burn our towns and distribute arms and poison to our slaves for the same purpose.

They have impoverished the slave-holding States by unequal and partial legislation, thereby enriching themselves by draining our substance.

They have refused to vote appropriations for protecting Texas against ruthless savages, for the sole reason that she is a slave-holding State.

And, finally, by the combined sectional vote of the seventeen non-slave-holding States, they have elected as president and vice-president of the whole confederacy two men whose chief claims to such high positions are their approval of these long continued wrongs, and their pledges to continue them to the final consummation of these schemes for the ruin of the slave-holding States.

In view of these and many other facts, it is meet that our own views should be distinctly proclaimed.

We hold as undeniable truths that the governments of the various States, and of the confederacy itself, were established exclusively by the white race, for themselves and their posterity; that the African race had no agency in their establishment; that they were rightfully held and regarded as an inferior and dependent race, and in that condition only could their existence in this country be rendered beneficial or tolerable.

That in this free government all white men are and of right ought to be entitled to equal civil and political rights; that the servitude of the African race, as existing in these States, is mutually beneficial to both bond and free, and is abundantly authorized and justified by the experience of mankind, and the revealed will of the Almighty Creator, as recognized by all Christian nations; while the destruction of the existing relations between the two races, as advocated by our sectional enemies, would bring inevitable calamities upon both and desolation upon the fifteen slave-holding states.

By the secession of six of the slave-holding States, and the certainty that others will speedily do likewise, Texas has no alternative but to remain in an isolated connection with the North, or unite her destinies with the South.

For these and other reasons, solemnly asserting that the federal constitution has been violated and virtually abrogated by the several States named, seeing that the federal government is now passing under the control of our enemies to be diverted from the exalted objects of its creation to those of oppression and wrong, and realizing that our own State can no longer look for protection, but to God and her own sons-- We the delegates of the people of Texas, in Convention assembled, have passed an ordinance dissolving all political connection with the government of the United States of America and the people thereof and confidently appeal to the intelligence and patriotism of the freemen of Texas to ratify the same at the ballot box, on the 23rd day of the present month.

Adopted in Convention on the 2nd day of Feby, in the year of our Lord one thousand eight hundred and sixty-one and of the independence of Texas the twenty-fifth.

A Declaration of the Immediate Causes which Induce and Justify the Secession of the State of Mississippi from the Federal Union.

In the momentous step which our State has taken of dissolving its connection with the government of which we so long formed a part, it is but just that we should declare the prominent reasons which have induced our course.

Our position is thoroughly identified with the institution of slavery-- the greatest material interest of the world. Its labor supplies the product which constitutes by far the largest and most important portions of commerce of the earth. These products are peculiar to the climate verging on the tropical regions, and by an imperious law of nature, none but the black race can bear exposure to the tropical sun. These products have become necessities of the world, and a blow at slavery is a blow at commerce and civilization. That blow has been long aimed at the institution, and was at the point of reaching its consummation. There was no choice left us but submission to the mandates of abolition, or a dissolution of the Union, whose principles had been subverted to work out our ruin.

That we do not overstate the dangers to our institution, a reference to a few facts will sufficiently prove.

The hostility to this institution commenced before the adoption of the Constitution, and was manifested in the well-known Ordinance of 1787, in regard to the Northwestern Territory.

The feeling increased, until, in 1819-20, it deprived the South of more than half the vast territory acquired from France.

The same hostility dismembered Texas and seized upon all the territory acquired from Mexico.

It has grown until it denies the right of property in slaves, and refuses protection to that right on the high seas, in the Territories, and wherever the government of the United States had jurisdiction.

It refuses the admission of new slave States into the Union, and seeks to extinguish it by confining it within its present limits, denying the power of expansion.

It tramples the original equality of the South under foot.

It has nullified the Fugitive Slave Law in almost every free State in the Union, and has utterly broken the compact which our fathers pledged their faith to maintain.

It advocates negro equality, socially and politically, and promotes insurrection and incendiarism in our midst.

It has enlisted its press, its pulpit and its schools against us, until the whole popular mind of the North is excited and inflamed with prejudice.

It has made combinations and formed associations to carry out its schemes of emancipation in the States and wherever else slavery exists.

It seeks not to elevate or to support the slave, but to destroy his present condition without providing a better.

It has invaded a State, and invested with the honors of martyrdom the wretch whose purpose was to apply flames to our dwellings, and the weapons of destruction to our lives.

It has broken every compact into which it has entered for our security.

It has given indubitable evidence of its design to ruin our agriculture, to prostrate our industrial pursuits and to destroy our social system.

It knows no relenting or hesitation in its purposes; it stops not in its march of aggression, and leaves us no room to hope for cessation or for pause.

It has recently obtained control of the Government, by the prosecution of its unhallowed schemes, and destroyed the last expectation of living together in friendship and brotherhood.

Utter subjugation awaits us in the Union, if we should consent longer to remain in it. It is not a matter of choice, but of necessity. We must either submit to degradation, and to the loss of property worth four billions of money, or we must secede from the Union framed by our fathers, to secure this as well as every other species of property. For far less cause than this, our fathers separated from the Crown of England.

Our decision is made. We follow their footsteps. We embrace the alternative of separation; and for the reasons here stated, we resolve to maintain our rights with the full consciousness of the justice of our course, and the undoubting belief of our ability to maintain it.

Constitution of the Confederate States; March 11, 1861

Preamble

We, the people of the Confederate States, each State acting in its
sovereign and independent character, in order to form a permanent
federal government, establish justice, insure domestic tranquillity, and
secure the blessings of liberty to ourselves and our posterity invoking
the favor and guidance of Almighty God do ordain and establish this
Constitution for the Confederate States of America.

Article I

Section I. All legislative powers herein delegated shall be vested in a
Congress of the Confederate States, which shall consist of a Senate and
House of Representatives.

Sec. 2. (I) The House of Representatives shall be composed of
members chosen every second year by the people of the several States;
and the electors in each State shall be citizens of the Confederate
States, and have the qualifications requisite for electors of the most
numerous branch of the State Legislature; but no person of foreign
birth, not a citizen of the Confederate States, shall be allowed to vote
for any officer, civil or political, State or Federal.

(2) No person shall be a Representative who shall not have attained the
age of twenty-five years, and be a citizen of the Confederate States, and
who shall not when elected, be an inhabitant of that State in which he
shall be chosen.

(3) Representatives and direct taxes shall be apportioned among the
several States, which may be included within this Confederacy,
according to their respective numbers, which shall be determined by
adding to the whole number of free persons, including those bound to
service for a term of years, and excluding Indians not taxed, three-
fifths of all slaves. ,The actual enumeration shall be made within three

years after the first meeting of the Congress of the Confederate States, and within every subsequent term of ten years, in such manner as they shall by law direct. The number of Representatives shall not exceed one for every fifty thousand, but each State shall have at least one Representative; and until such enumeration shall be made, the State of South Carolina shall be entitled to choose six; the State of Georgia ten; the State of Alabama nine; the State of Florida two; the State of Mississippi seven; the State of Louisiana six; and the State of Texas six.

(4) When vacancies happen in the representation from any State the executive authority thereof shall issue writs of election to fill such vacancies.

(5) The House of Representatives shall choose their Speaker and other officers; and shall have the sole power of impeachment; except that any judicial or other Federal officer, resident and acting solely within the limits of any State, may be impeached by a vote of two-thirds of both branches of the Legislature thereof.

Sec. 3. (I) The Senate of the Confederate States shall be composed of two Senators from each State, chosen for six years by the Legislature thereof, at the regular session next immediately preceding the commencement of the term of service; and each Senator shall have one vote.

(2) Immediately after they shall be assembled, in consequence of the first election, they shall be divided as equally as may be into three classes. The seats of the Senators of the first class shall be vacated at the expiration of the second year; of the second class at the expiration of the fourth year; and of the third class at the expiration of the sixth year; so that one-third may be chosen every second year; and if vacancies happen by resignation, or other wise, during the recess of the Legislature of any State, the Executive thereof may make temporary appointments until the next meeting of the Legislature, which shall then fill such vacancies.

(3) No person shall be a Senator who shall not have attained the age of thirty years, and be a citizen of the Confederate States; and who shall not, then elected, be an inhabitant of the State for which he shall be chosen.

(4) The Vice President of the Confederate States shall be president of the Senate, but shall have no vote unless they be equally divided.

(5) The Senate shall choose their other officers; and also a president pro tempore in the absence of the Vice President, or when he shall exercise the office of President of the Confederate states.

(6) The Senate shall have the sole power to try all impeachments. When sitting for that purpose, they shall be on oath or affirmation. When the President of the Confederate States is tried, the Chief Justice shall preside; and no person shall be convicted without the concurrence of two-thirds of the members present.

(7) Judgment in cases of impeachment shall not extend further than to removal from office, and disqualification to hold any office of honor, trust, or profit under the Confederate States; but the party convicted shall, nevertheless, be liable and subject to indictment, trial, judgment, and punishment according to law.

Sec. 4. (I) The times, places, and manner of holding elections for Senators and Representatives shall be prescribed in each State by the Legislature thereof, subject to the provisions of this Constitution; but the Congress may, at any time, by law, make or alter such regulations, except as to the times and places of choosing Senators.

(2) The Congress shall assemble at least once in every year; and such meeting shall be on the first Monday in December, unless they shall, by law, appoint a different day.

Sec. 5. (I) Each House shall be the judge of the elections, returns, and qualifications of its own members, and a majority of each shall constitute a quorum to do business; but a smaller number may adjourn from day to day, and may be authorized to compel the attendance of absent members, in such manner and under such penalties as each House may provide.

(2) Each House may determine the rules of its proceedings, punish its members for disorderly behavior, and, with the concurrence of two-thirds of the whole number, expel a member.

(3) Each House shall keep a journal of its proceedings, and from time to time publish the same, excepting such parts as may in their judgment require secrecy; and the yeas and nays of the members of either House, on any question, shall, at the desire of one-fifth of those present, be entered on the journal.

(4) Neither House, during the session of Congress, shall, without the consent of the other, adjourn for more than three days, nor to any other place than that in which the two Houses shall be sitting.

Sec. 6. (I) The Senators and Representatives shall receive a compensation for their services, to be ascertained by law, and paid out of the Treasury of the Confederate States. They shall, in all cases, except treason, felony, and breach of the peace, be privileged from arrest during their attendance at the session of their respective Houses, and in going to and returning from the same; and for any speech or debate in either House, they shall not be questioned in any other place. 'o Senator or Representative shall, during the time for which he was elected, be appointed to any civil office under the authority of the Confederate States, which shall have been created, or the emoluments whereof shall have been increased during such time; and no person holding any office under the Confederate States shall be a member of either House during his continuance in office. But Congress may, by law, grant to the principal officer in each of the Executive Departments a seat upon the floor of either House, with the privilege of discussing any measures appertaining to his department.

Sec. 7. (I) All bills for raising revenue shall originate in the House of Representatives; but the Senate may propose or concur with amendments, as on other bills.

(2) Every bill which shall have passed both Houses, shall, before it becomes a law, be presented to the President of the Confederate States; if he approve, he shall sign it; but if not, he shall return it, with his objections, to that House in which it shall have originated, who shall enter the objections at large on their journal, and proceed to reconsider it. If, after such reconsideration, two-thirds of that House shall agree to pass the bill, it shall be sent, together with the objections, to the other House, by which it shall likewise be reconsidered, and if approved by two-thirds of that House, it shall become a law. But in all such cases, the votes of both Houses shall be determined by yeas and nays, and the names of the persons voting for and against the bill shall be entered on the journal of each House respective}y. If any bill shall not be returned by the President within ten days (Sundays excepted) after it shall have been presented to him, the same shall be a law, in like manner as if he had signed it, unless the Congress, by their adjournment, prevent its return; in which case it shall not be a law. The President may approve any appropriation and disapprove any other appropriation in the same bill. In such case he shall, in signing the bill, designate the appropriations disapproved; and shall return a copy of such appropriations, with his objections, to the House in which the bill shall have originated; and the same proceedings shall then be had as in case of other bills disapproved by the President.

(3) Every order, resolution, or vote, to which the concurrence of both Houses may be necessary (except on a question of adjournment) shall be presented to the President of the Confederate States; and before the same shall take effect, shall be approved by him; or, being disapproved by him, shall be repassed by two-thirds of both Houses, according to the rules and limitations prescribed in case of a bill.

Sec. 8. The Congress shall have power-

(I) To lay and collect taxes, duties, imposts, and excises for revenue, necessary to pay the debts, provide for the common defense, and carry on the Government of the Confederate States; but no bounties shall be granted from the Treasury; nor shall any duties or taxes on importations from foreign nations be laid to promote or foster any branch of industry; and all duties, imposts, and excises shall be uniform throughout the Confederate States.

(2) To borrow money on the credit of the Confederate States.

(3) To regulate commerce with foreign nations, and among the several States, and with the Indian tribes; but neither this, nor any other clause contained in the Constitution, shall ever be construed to delegate the power to Congress to appropriate money for any internal improvement intended to facilitate commerce; except for the purpose of furnishing lights, beacons, and buoys, and other aids to navigation upon the coasts, and the improvement of harbors and the removing of obstructions in river navigation; in all which cases such duties shall be laid on the navigation facilitated thereby as may be necessary to pay the costs and expenses thereof.

(4) To establish uniform laws of naturalization, and uniform laws on the subject of bankruptcies, throughout the Confederate States; but no law of Congress shall discharge any debt contracted before the passage of the same.

(5) To coin money, regulate the value thereof, and of foreign coin, and fix the standard of weights and measures.

(6) To provide for the punishment of counterfeiting the securities and current coin of the Confederate States.

(7) To establish post offices and post routes; but the expenses of the Post Office Department, after the 1st day of March in the year of our Lord eighteen hundred and sixty-three, shall be paid out of its own revenues.

(8) To promote the progress of science and useful arts, by securing for limited times to authors and inventors the exclusive right to their respective writings and discoveries.

(9) To constitute tribunals inferior to the Supreme Court.

(10) To define and punish piracies and felonies committed on the high seas, and offenses against the law of nations.

(11) To declare war, grant letters of marque and reprisal, and make rules concerning captures on land and water.

(12) To raise and support armies; but no appropriation of money to that use shall be for a longer term than two years.

(13) To provide and maintain a navy.

(14) To make rules for the government and regulation of the land and naval forces.

(15) To provide for calling forth the militia to execute the laws of the Confederate States, suppress insurrections, and repel invasions.

(16) To provide for organizing, arming, and disciplining the militia, and for governing such part of them as may be employed in the service of the Confederate States; reserving to the States, respectively, the appointment of the officers, and the authority of training the militia according to the discipline prescribed by Congress.

(17) To exercise exclusive legislation, in all cases whatsoever, over such district (not exceeding ten miles square) as may, by cession of one or more States and the acceptance of Congress, become the seat of the Government of the Confederate States; and to exercise like authority over all places purchased by the consent of the Legislature of the State

in which the same shall be, for the . erection of forts, magazines, arsenals, dockyards, and other needful buildings; and

(18) To make all laws which shall be necessary and proper for carrying into execution the foregoing powers, and all other powers vested by this Constitution in the Government of the Confederate States, or in any department or officer thereof.

Sec. 9. (I) The importation of negroes of the African race from any foreign country other than the slaveholding States or Territories of the United States of America, is hereby forbidden; and Congress is required to pass such laws as shall effectually prevent the same.

(2) Congress shall also have power to prohibit the introduction of slaves from any State not a member of, or Territory not belonging to, this Confederacy.

(3) The privilege of the writ of habeas corpus shall not be suspended, unless when in cases of rebellion or invasion the public safety may require it.

(4) No bill of attainder, ex post facto law, or law denying or impairing the right of property in negro slaves shall be passed.

(5) No capitation or other direct tax shall be laid, unless in proportion to the census or enumeration hereinbefore directed to be taken.

(6) No tax or duty shall be laid on articles exported from any State, except by a vote of two-thirds of both Houses.

(7) No preference shall be given by any regulation of commerce or revenue to the ports of one State over those of another.

(8) No money shall be drawn from the Treasury, but in consequence of appropriations made by law; and a regular statement and account of

the receipts and expenditures of all public money shall be published from time to time.

(9) Congress shall appropriate no money from the Treasury except by a vote of two-thirds of both Houses, taken by yeas and nays, unless it be asked and estimated for by some one of the heads of departments and submitted to Congress by the President; or for the purpose of paying its own expenses and contingencies; or for the payment of claims against the Confederate States, the justice of which shall have been judicially declared by a tribunal for the investigation of claims against the Government, which it is hereby made the duty of Congress to establish.

(10) All bills appropriating money shall specify in Federal currency the exact amount of each appropriation and the purposes for which it is made; and Congress shall grant no extra compensation to any public contractor, officer, agent, or servant, after such contract shall have been made or such service rendered.

(11) No title of nobility shall be granted by the Confederate States; and no person holding any office of profit or trust under them shall, without the consent of the Congress, accept of any present, emolument, office, or title of any kind whatever, from any king, prince, or foreign state.

(12) Congress shall make no law respecting an establishment of religion, or prohibiting the free exercise thereof; or abridging the freedom of speech, or of the press; or the right of the people peaceably to assemble and petition the Government for a redress of grievances.

(13) A well-regulated militia being necessary to the security of a free State, the right of the people to keep and bear arms shall not be infringed.

(14) No soldier shall, in time of peace, be quartered in any house without the consent of the owner; nor in time of war, but in a manner to be prescribed by law.

(15) The right of the people to be secure in their persons, houses, papers, and effects, against unreasonable searches and seizures, shall not be violated; and no warrants shall issue but upon probable cause, supported by oath or affirmation, and particularly describing the place to be searched and the persons or things to be seized.

(16) No person shall be held to answer for a capital or otherwise infamous crime, unless on a presentment or indictment of a grand jury, except in cases arising in the land or naval forces, or in the militia, when in actual service in time of war or public danger; nor shall any person be subject for the same offense to be twice put in jeopardy of life or limb; nor be compelled, in any criminal case, to be a witness against himself; nor be deprived of life, liberty, or property without due process of law; nor shall private property be taken for public use, without just compensation.

(17) In all criminal prosecutions the accused shall enjoy the right to a speedy and public trial, by an impartial jury of the State and district wherein the crime shall have been committed, which district shall have been previously ascertained by law, and to be informed of the nature and cause of the accusation; to be confronted with the witnesses against him; to have compulsory process for obtaining witnesses in his favor; and to have the assistance of counsel for his defense.

(18) In suits at common law, where the value in controversy shall exceed twenty dollars, the right of trial by jury shall be preserved; and no fact so tried by a jury shall be otherwise reexamined in any court of the Confederacy, than according to the rules of common law.

(19) Excessive bail shall not be required, nor excessive fines imposed, nor cruel and unusual punishments inflicted.

(20) Every law, or resolution having the force of law, shall relate to but one subject, and that shall be expressed in the title.

Sec. 10. (I) No State shall enter into any treaty, alliance, or confederation; grant letters of marque and reprisal; coin money; make anything but gold and silver coin a tender in payment of debts; pass any bill of attainder, or ex post facto law, or law impairing the obligation of contracts; or grant any title of nobility.

(2) No State shall, without the consent of the Congress, lay any imposts or duties on imports or exports, except what may be absolutely necessary for executing its inspection laws; and the net produce of all duties and imposts, laid by any State on imports, or exports, shall be for the use of the Treasury of the Confederate States; and all such laws shall be subject to the revision and control of Congress.

(3) No State shall, without the consent of Congress, lay any duty on tonnage, except on seagoing vessels, for the improvement of its rivers and harbors navigated by the said vessels; but such duties shall not conflict with any treaties of the Confederate States with foreign nations; and any surplus revenue thus derived shall, after making such improvement, be paid into the common treasury. Nor shall any State keep troops or ships of war in time of peace, enter into any agreement or compact with another State, or with a foreign power, or engage in war, unless actually invaded, or in such imminent danger as will not admit of delay. But when any river divides or flows through two or more States they may enter into compacts with each other to improve the navigation thereof.

ARTICLE II

Section I. (I) The executive power shall be vested in a President of the Confederate States of America. He and the Vice President shall hold their offices for the term of six years; but the President shall not be reeligible. The President and Vice President shall be elected as follows:

(2) Each State shall appoint, in such manner as the Legislature thereof may direct, a number of electors equal to the whole number of Senators and Representatives to which the State may be entitled in the Congress; but no Senator or Representative or person holding an office of trust or profit under the Confederate States shall be appointed an elector.

(3) The electors shall meet in their respective States and vote by ballot for President and Vice President, one of whom, at least, shall not be an inhabitant of the same State with themselves; they shall name in their ballots the person voted for as President, and in distinct ballots the person voted for as Vice President, and they shall make distinct lists of all persons voted for as President, and of all persons voted for as Vice President, and of the number of votes for each, which lists they shall sign and certify, and transmit, sealed, to the seat of the Government of. the Confederate States, directed to the President of the Senate; the President of the Senate shall,in the presence of the Senate and House of Representatives, open all the certificates, and the votes shall then be counted; the person having the greatest number of votes for President shall be the President, if such number be a majority of the whole number of electors appointed; and if no person have such majority, then from the persons having the highest numbers, not exceeding three, on the list of those voted for as President, the House of Representatives shall choose immediately, by ballot, the President. But in choosing the President the votes shall be taken by States, the representation from each State having one vote; a quorum for this purpose shall consist of a member or members from two-thirds of the States, and a majority of all the States shall be necessary to a choice. And if the House of Representatives shall not choose a President, whenever the right of choice shall devolve upon them, before the 4th day of March next following, then the Vice President shall act as President, as in case of the death, or other constitutional disability of the President.

(4) The person having the greatest number of votes as Vice President shall be the Vice President, if such number be a majority of the whole number of electors appointed; and if no person have a majority, then, from the two highest numbers on the list, the Senate shall choose the Vice President; a quorum for the purpose shall consist of two-thirds of the whole number of Senators, and a majority of the whole number shall be necessary to a choice.

(5) But no person constitutionally ineligible to the office of President shall be eligible to that of Vice President of the Confederate States.

(6) The Congress may determine the time of choosing the electors, and the day on which they shall give their votes; which day shall be the same throughout the Confederate States.

(7) No person except a natural-born citizen of the Confederate; States, or a citizen thereof at the time of the adoption of this Constitution, or a citizen thereof born in the United States prior to the 20th of December, 1860, shall be eligible to the office of President; neither shall any person be eligible to that office who shall not have attained the age of thirty-five years, and been fourteen years a resident within the limits of the Confederate States, as they may exist at the time of his election.

(8) In case of the removal of the President from office, or of his death, resignation, or inability to discharge the powers and duties of said office, the same shall devolve on the Vice President; and the Congress may, by law, provide for the case of removal, death, resignation, or inability, both of the President and Vice President, declaring what officer shall then act as President; and such officer shall act accordingly until the disability be removed or a President shall be elected.

(9) The President shall, at stated times, receive for his services a compensation, which shall neither be increased nor diminished during the period for which he shall have been elected; and he shall not

receive within that period any other emolument from the Confederate States, or any of them.

(10) Before he enters on the execution of his office he shall take the following oath or affirmation:

Sec. 2. (I) The President shall be Commander-in-Chief of the Army and Navy of the Confederate States, and of the militia of the several States, when called into the actual service of the Confederate States; he may require the opinion, in writing, of the principal officer in each of the Executive Departments, upon any subject relating to the duties of their respective offices; and he shall have power to grant reprieves and pardons for offenses against the Confederate States, except in cases of impeachment.

(2) He shall have power, by and with the advice and consent of the Senate, to make treaties; provided two-thirds of the Senators present concur; and he shall nominate, and by and with the advice and consent of the Senate shall appoint, ambassadors, other public ministers and consuls, judges of the Supreme Court, and all other officers of the Confederate States whose appointments are not herein otherwise provided for, and which shall be established by law; but the Congress may, by law, vest the appointment of such inferior officers, as they think proper, in the President alone, in the courts of law, or in the heads of departments.

(3) The principal officer in each of the Executive Departments, and all persons connected with the diplomatic service, may be removed from office at the pleasure of the President. All other civil officers of the Executive Departments may be removed at any time by the President, or other appointing power, when their services are unnecessary, or for dishonesty, incapacity. inefficiency, misconduct, or neglect of duty; and when so removed, the removal shall be reported to the Senate, together with the reasons therefor.

(4) The President shall have power to fill all vacancies that may happen during the recess of the Senate, by granting commissions which shall expire at the end of their next session; but no person rejected by the Senate shall be reappointed to the same office during their ensuing recess.

Sec. 3. (I) The President shall, from time to time, give to the Congress information of the state of the Confederacy, and recommend to their consideration such measures as he shall judge necessary and expedient; he may, on extraordinary occasions, convene both Houses, or either of them; and in case of disagreement between them, with respect to the time of adjournment, he may adjourn them to such time as he shall think proper; he shall receive ambassadors and other public ministers; he shall take care that the laws be faithfully executed, and shall commission all the officers of the Confederate States.

Sec. 4. (I) The President, Vice President, and all civil officers of the Confederate States, shall be removed from office on impeachment for and conviction of treason, bribery, or other high crimes and misdemeanors.

ARTICLE III

Section I. (I) The judicial power of the Confederate States shall be vested in one Supreme Court, and in such inferior courts as the Congress may, from time to time, ordain and establish. The judges, both of the Supreme and inferior courts, shall hold their offices during good behavior, and shall, at stated times, receive for their services a compensation which shall not be diminished during their continuance in office.

Sec. 2. (I) The judicial power shall extend to all cases arising under this Constitution, the laws of the Confederate States, and treaties made, or which shall be made, under their authority; to all cases affecting ambassadors, other public ministers and consuls; to all cases of admiralty and maritime jurisdiction; to controversies to which the

Confederate States shall be a party; to controversies between two or more States; between a State and citizens of another State, where the State is plaintiff; between citizens claiming lands under grants of different States; and between a State or the citizens thereof, and foreign states, citizens, or subjects; but no State shall be sued by a citizen or subject of any foreign state.

(2) In all cases affecting ambassadors, other public ministers and consuls, and those in which a State shall be a party, the Supreme Court shall have original jurisdiction. In all the other cases before mentioned, the Supreme Court shall have appellate jurisdiction both as to law and fact, with such exceptions and under such regulations as the Congress shall make.

(3) The trial of all crimes, except in cases of impeachment, shall be by jury, and such trial shall be held in the State where the said crimes shall have been committed; but when not committed within any State, the trial shall be at such place or places as the Congress may by law have directed.

Sec. 3. (I) Treason against the Confederate States shall consist only in levying war against.them, or in adhering to their enemies, giving them aid and comfort. No person shall be convicted of treason unless on the testimony of two witnesses to the same overt act, or on confession in open court.

(2) The Congress shall have power to declare the punishment of treason; but no attainder of treason shall work corruption of blood, or forfeiture, except during the life of the person attainted.

ARTICLE IV

Section I. (I) Full faith and credit shall be given in each State to the public acts, records, and judicial proceedings of every other State; and the Congress may, by general laws, prescribe the manner in which such acts, records, and proceedings shall be proved, and the effect thereof.

Sec. 2. (I) The citizens of each State shall be entitled to all the privileges and immunities of citizens in the several States; and shall have the right of transit and sojourn in any State of this Confederacy, with their slaves and other property; and the right of property in said slaves shall not be thereby impaired.

(2) A person charged in any State with treason, felony, or other crime against the laws of such State, who shall flee from justice, and be found in another State, shall, on demand of the executive authority of the State from which he fled, be delivered up, to be removed to the State having jurisdiction of the crime.

(3) No slave or other person held to service or labor in any State or Territory of the Confederate States, under the laws thereof, escaping or lawfully carried into another, shall, in consequence of any law or regulation therein, be discharged from such service or labor; but shall be delivered up on claim of the party to whom such slave belongs,. or to whom such service or labor may be due.

Sec. 3. (I) Other States may be admitted into this Confederacy by a vote of two-thirds of the whole House of Representatives and two-thirds of the Senate, the Senate voting by States; but no new State shall be formed or erected within the jurisdiction of any other State, nor any State be formed by the junction of two or more States, or parts of States, without the consent of the Legislatures of the States concerned, as well as of the Congress.

(2) The Congress shall have power to dispose of and make allneedful rules and regulations concerning the property of the Confederate States, including the lands thereof.

(3) The Confederate States may acquire new territory; and Congress shall have power to legislate and provide governments for the inhabitants of all territory belonging to the Confederate States, lying without the limits of the several Sates; and may permit them, at such

times, and in such manner as it may by law provide, to form States to
be admitted into the Confederacy. In all such territory the institution
of negro slavery, as it now exists in the Confederate States, shall be
recognized and protected be Congress and by the Territorial
government; and the inhabitants of the several Confederate States and
Territories shall have the right to take to such Territory any slaves
lawfully held by them in any of the States or Territories of the
Confederate States.

(4) The Confederate States shall guarantee to every State that now is,
or hereafter may become, a member of this Confederacy, a republican
form of government; and shall protect each of them against invasion;
and on application of the Legislature or of the Executive when the
Legislature is not in session) against domestic violence.

ARTICLE V

Section I. (I) Upon the demand of any three States, legally assembled
in their several conventions, the Congress shall summon a convention
of all the States, to take into consideration such amendments to the
Constitution as the said States shall concur in suggesting at the time
when the said demand is made; and should any of the proposed
amendments to the Constitution be agreed on by the said convention,
voting by States, and the same be ratified by the Legislatures of two-
thirds of the several States, or by conventions in two-thirds thereof, as
the one or the other mode of ratification may be proposed by the
general convention, they shall thenceforward form a part of this
Constitution. But no State shall, without its consent, be deprived of its
equal representation in the Senate.

ARTICLE VI

I. The Government established by this Constitution is the successor of
the Provisional Government of the Confederate States of America, and
all the laws passed by the latter shall continue in force until the same
shall be repealed or modified; and all the officers appointed by the

same shall remain in office until their successors are appointed and qualified, or the offices abolished.

2. All debts contracted and engagements entered into before the adoption of this Constitution shall be as valid against the Confederate States under this Constitution, as under the Provisional Government.

3. This Constitution, and the laws of the Confederate States made in pursuance thereof, and all treaties made, or which shall be made, under the authority of the Confederate States, shall be the supreme law of the land; and the judges in every State shall be bound thereby, anything in the constitution or laws of any State to the contrary notwithstanding.

4. The Senators and Representatives before mentioned, and the members of the several State Legislatures, and all executive and judicial officers, both of the Confederate States and of the several States, shall be bound by oath or affirmation to support this Constitution; but no religious test shall ever be required as a qualification to any office or public trust under the Confederate States.

5. The enumeration, in the Constitution, of certain rights shall not be construed to deny or disparage others retained by the people of the several States.

6. The powers not delegated to the Confederate States by the Constitution, nor prohibited by it to the States, are reserved to the States, respectively, or to the people thereof.

ARTICLE VII

I. The ratification of the conventions of five States shall be sufficient for the establishment of this Constitution between the States so ratifying the same.

2. When five States shall have ratified this Constitution, in the manner before specified, the Congress under the Provisional Constitution shall

prescribe the time for holding the election of President and Vice President; and for the meeting of the Electoral College; and for counting the votes, and inaugurating the President. They shall, also, prescribe the time for holding the first election of members of Congress under this Constitution, and the time for assembling the same. Until the assembling of such Congress, the Congress under the Provisional Constitution shall continue to exercise the legislative powers granted them; not extending beyond the time limited by the Constitution of the Provisional Government.

Adopted unanimously by the Congress of the Confederate States of South Carolina, Georgia, Florida, Alabama, Mississippi, Louisiana, and Texas, sitting in convention at the capitol, the city of Montgomery, Ala., on the eleventh day of March, in the year eighteen hundred and Sixty-one.

HOWELL COBB, President of the Congress.

South Carolina: R. Barnwell Rhett, C. G. Memminger, Wm. Porcher Miles, James Chesnut, Jr., R. W. Barnwell, William W. Boyce, Lawrence M. Keitt, T. J. Withers.

Georgia: Francis S. Bartow, Martin J. Crawford, Benjamin H. Hill, Thos. R. R. Cobb.

Florida: Jackson Morton, J. Patton Anderson, Jas. B. Owens.

Alabama: Richard W. Walker, Robt. H. Smith, Colin J. McRae, William P. Chilton, Stephen F. Hale, David P. Lewis, Tho. Fearn, Jno. Gill Shorter, J. L. M. Curry.

Mississippi: Alex. M. Clayton, James T. Harrison, William S. Barry, W. S. Wilson, Walker Brooke, W. P. Harris, J. A. P. Campbell.

Louisiana: Alex. de Clouet, C. M. Conrad, Duncan F. Kenner, Henry Marshall.

Texas: John Hemphill, Thomas N. Waul, John H. Reagan, Williamson
S. Oldham, Louis T. Wigfall, John Gregg, William Beck Ochiltree.